OECD ECONOMIC SURVEYS

GERMANY

ORGANISATION FOR ECONOMIC CO-OPERATION AND DEVELOPMENT

2649956

ORGANISATION FOR ECONOMIC CO-OPERATION AND DEVELOPMENT

Pursuant to Article 1 of the Convention signed in Paris on 14th December 1960, and which came into force on 30th September 1961, the Organisation for Economic Co-operation and Development (OECD) shall promote policies designed:

— to achieve the highest sustainable economic growth and employment and a rising standard of living in Member countries, while maintaining financial stability, and thus to contribute to the development of the world economy;
— to contribute to sound economic expansion in Member as well as non-member countries in the process of economic development; and
— to contribute to the expansion of world trade on a multilateral, non-discriminatory basis in accordance with international obligations.

The original Member countries of the OECD are Austria, Belgium, Canada, Denmark, France, Germany, Greece, Iceland, Ireland, Italy, Luxembourg, the Netherlands, Norway, Portugal, Spain, Sweden, Switzerland, Turkey, the United Kingdom and the United States. The following countries became Members subsequently through accession at the dates indicated hereafter: Japan (28th April 1964), Finland (28th January 1969), Australia (7th June 1971) and New Zealand (29th May 1973). The Commission of the European Communities takes part in the work of the OECD (Article 13 of the OECD Convention). Yugoslavia has a special status at OECD (agreement of 28th October 1961).

Publié également en français.

Contents

Introduction   9

I.   On the road to integration   12

  1991 in retrospect: summary of annual projections and outcomes   13
  Demand and output growth weakened through 1991   14
    Trends in demand   14
    Stagnating output and falling productivity   20
  The labour market: falling unemployment in the west – falling
    employment in the east   22
  An intensifying cost-price spiral   24
  Turnaround of the current external account   27

II. Efforts to safeguard macroeconomic stability   30

  Fiscal policy: striving to contain borrowing requirements   30
    1991: higher spending pressure met with higher taxation   31
    Better-than-expected outcomes for 1991   31
    Higher public sector deficit in prospect for 1992   34
  Rising public transfers to the new Länder   35
  Public sector borrowing requirements   38
  Medium-term fiscal consolidation   41
  Monetary policy: the quest for financial stability   43
    Accelerating monetary growth despite higher interest rates   46
    Foreign exchange and capital market developments   48
  Structural policies: selected issues   48
    Subsidy cutting: difficult first steps   48
    Privatisation   52

III.	**The present situation and projections to 1993**	55
	Policy assumptions	57
	Fiscal policy: efforts to reduce public sector deficits	57
	No let-up in the anti-inflationary stance of monetary policy	57
	The outlook to 1993	58
IV.	**The labour market after unification**	63
	The development of labour market institutions in western Germany	65
	Collective bargaining and co-determination	65
	Contract enforcement and extension	66
	Education, training and active labour market measures	67
	Strikes, employment protection and social security	69
	The labour market situation and adjustment in eastern Germany	71
	Convergence through the market?	71
	Wage determination - collective bargaining and the social partners	74
	Convergence and catch-up settlements	76
	Social security and employment creation measures	80
	Overview	85
V.	**Conclusions**	86
	Notes and references	94
	Annex	
	Chronology of main economic events	101
	Statistical and structural annex	105

Tables

Text

1.	Projections and outcomes for western Germany, 1991	14
2.	Domestic demand and GNP growth, western Germany	15
3.	Appropriation account for households, western Germany	16

4. Change in real net goods and services exports, western Germany 19
5. Comparative statistics: eastern and western Germany, 1991 21
6. The western German labour market 22
7. The labour market in the eastern Länder 23
8. Exports and competitiveness 27
9. Components of the current account of the balance of payments 28
10. The capital account 29
11. General government appropriation account 33
12. The federal budget 35
13. The Unity Fund 38
14. Components of public-sector financial balance 39
15. The federal government medium-term financial plan 41
16. Monetary targeting for 1992 46
17. Subsidisation 51
18. Labour shedding in Treuhandanstalt firms 1990-1991 53
19. Projections to 1993 59
20. International competitiveness, market growth and export performance 60
21. Expenditure on labour market measures 69

Statistical annex

A. Selected background statistics 104
B. Gross domestic product by origin 108
C. Gross national product by demand components 109
D. Distribution of national income 110
E. Receipts and expenditure of general government: national accounts basis 111
F. Balance of payments 112
G. Imports and exports by regions – customs basis 114
H. Foreign trade by main commodity groups – customs basis 116
I. Money and credit 117
J. Population and employment 118
K. Wages and prices 119

Structural annex

L.   Structure of output and performance indicators   120
M.   Labour market indicators   121
N.   Public sector   122
O.   Financial markets   123

Diagrams

1.   Retail turnover and consumer confidence, western Germany   17
2.   Investment spending, western Germany   19
3.   Real GDP in eastern and western Germany, 1989-1991   20
4.   Cost and price developments, western Germany   25
5.   Trends in general government spending, taxation and financial balance   32
6.   Sources and uses of transfers to the eastern Länder 1992   37
7.   Public sector indebtedness   42
8.   Money market developments   44
9.   Money supply developments   47
10.   Foreign exchange rate developments and interest-rate differentials   49
11.   The yield structure in the bond market   50
12.   Status of Treuhandanstalt firms   53
13.   The eastern German labour force   64
14.   The German labour force and unemployment by level of qualification   75
15.   The eastern German metal workers' catch-up settlement   76
16.   Tarif and effective wages in western and eastern Germany, by industry   78

BASIC STATISTICS OF GERMANY

THE LAND

			Million inhabitants
Area, 1990 (thousand sq.km)	356.9	Major cities, 30.06.1989	
Agricultural area, 1990 (thousand sq.km)	196.7		
Forests, 1990 (thousand sq.km)	103.9	Berlin	3.4
		Hamburg	1.6
		Munich	1.2
		Cologne	0.9
		Frankfurt	0.6
		Essen	0.6
		Dortmund	0.6
		Dusseldorf	0.6
		Stuttgart	0.6
		Leipzig	0.5

THE PEOPLE

Population, Dec. 1990	79 753 000	Labour force total, 1991[1]	30 575 000
Number of inhabitants per sq.km	222	Civilian employment, 1991[1]	28 430 000
		of which: Agriculture	927 000
Net natural increase in population, 1990	-12 404	Industry	11 160 000
Net migration, 1989[1]	+977 223	Other activities	16 343 000

PRODUCTION

GDP, 1991 (billions of DM)	2 782	Origin of GDP, 1991 (per cent):	
GDP per head, 1991 (US$)	21 009	Agriculture, forestry, fishing	1.3
Gross fixed investment (1991):		Industry (incl. construction)	38.4
per cent of GDP	23	Services	60.3
per head (US$)	4 849		

THE GOVERNMENT

			seats
Public consumption, 1991 (per cent of GDP)	16.9	Composition of Federal Parliament:	
		Social Democrats (SPD)	239
General government current revenue, 1991 (per cent of GDP)	42.1	Christian Democrats (CDU)	268
		Free Democrats (FDP)	79
Public debt end 1990 (ratio to general government current revenue)[1]	100.9	Christian Socialists (CSU)	51
		PDS	17
		B90/Greens	8

Last general election: 02.12.1990
Next general election: Autumn 1994

FOREIGN TRADE

Exports:		Imports:	
Exports of goods and services as per cent of GDP, 1991	29.6	Imports of goods and services as per cent of GDP, 1991	28.9
Main exports, 1991 (per cent of total merchandise exports):		Main imports, 1991 (per cent of total merchandise imports):	
Products of agriculture, forestry and fishing	1	Products of agriculture, forestry and fishing	5
Basic materials and semi-finished goods	24	Basic materials and semi-finished goods	28
Manufactured foods and tobacco	4	Manufactured foods and tobacco	6
Other consumer manufactures	13	Other consumer manufactures	17
Investment goods	56	Investment goods	41
Other exports	2	Other imports	3
Total	100	Total	100

THE CURRENCY

Monetary unit: Deutsche Mark	Currency units per US$, average of daily figures:	
	Year 1991	1.659
	April 1992	1.648

1. Excluding eastern Germany.
Note: An international comparison of certain basic statistics is given in an annex table.

This Survey is based on the Secretariat's study prepared for the annual review of Germany by the Economic and Development Review Committee on 26th May 1992.

•

After revisions in the light of discussions during the review, final approval of the Survey for publication was given by the Committee on 25th June 1992.

•

The previous Survey of Germany was issued in July 1991.

Introduction

The past two years have been challenging for the German economy. In the wake of the rapid political unification, the enlarged German economy has increasingly felt the strains of merging two economic regions with vastly different economic systems and performance. Policies have been subjected to two opposing pressures: on the one hand, to accelerate economic reconstruction in the new Länder and to provide adequate social support, and on the other, to safeguard domestic financial stability.

As discussed in last year's Survey, for the structurally-weak and run-down eastern German economy unification meant sudden entry into highly competitive world markets with a high real exchange rate upon conversion of its former currency and merger with an efficient, high-income country with consequent strong upward pressure on wages. The collapse of trade with former CMEA partners gave an additional shock to the eastern German economy. As a result, a complete collapse of production and employment could be avoided only by massive financial transfers. During the initial period after unification a substantial portion of the largely credit-financed support translated into higher demand for western German products. Besides, there was sizeable demand spill-over to the rest of the world as witnessed by the swing of the all-German current external account from high surplus into deficit. The stimulus thus provided to Germany's main trading partners was, however, damped by the resulting consequences on interest rates.

1991 saw turning points for both eastern German and western German output growth. In the east, the previously steep fall of production appears to have bottomed out by the middle of the year, but a broadly-based upswing has not yet developed. In the west, output peaked in the second quarter of 1991, when it was 5 per cent up on a year earlier, and it receded during the following two quarters: net real exports weakened, private consumption slowed after the introduction of

9

the "solidarity levy" and investment activity moderated in response to depressed business expectations and pressure on profits. For the year as a whole, the output contraction in the new Länder is estimated to have been more than 30 per cent, while in the old Länder real GDP increased on average almost 3½ per cent. The rapid increase of the labour supply in the west and the turnaround of the current external account moderated pressures on capacity, but the trend in underlying costs was firmly upwards. This reflected a virtual pause in the growth of western German labour productivity and, more importantly, a sharp increase in negotiated wage rates. Unemployment rose further in the eastern Länder, while continuing to decline in western Germany.

1992 seems set to be a difficult year for both parts of Germany: output may pick up strongly in the eastern Länder, but unemployment will be affected only with a considerable lag, given the speed with which wages are running ahead of productivity growth. Expansionary impulses are likely to come mainly from construction activity both in the private and in the public sector. In western Germany, the hoped-for recovery of exports may set in later than expected. But more importantly, the current tension between wage developments and stabilisation objectives will keep interest rates high and profits under pressure. However, helped by favourable weather conditions the decline in output in the second half of last year was more than made good for in the first quarter of this year and a modest upswing, driven mainly by tax-induced increases in private consumption, may be expected to develop later in 1992. With domestic demand growth subdued, inflation should moderate (abstracting from the effects of the VAT increase in 1993) and the current-account deficit may shrink. On these trends, unemployment could pick up in the old Länder, while the shedding of labour in eastern Germany should diminish.

Part I of the Survey reviews economic developments in the two parts of Germany since unification, seeking to identify the reasons why the integration process has been more disruptive and costly than widely thought at the outset. Part II discusses the difficult balancing of policies which has been called for by these developments. Part III presents projections until 1993, assessing both the prospects for a quick return to a path of price disinflation and budget consolidation and, for the eastern German economy, the chance of being put on a self-sustainable course of catching-up with the western Länder. Given the central role of wage developments both for cyclical developments in the west and for the speed and nature of the structural adjustment in the east, the special chapter of this Survey (Part IV) focuses on institutional and behavioural features of the labour market, with a view to gaining a better understanding of current wage-determining mechanisms. A summary of the key points of the Survey is provided in the Conclusions, which also offer some policy recommendations.

I. On the road to integration

Two years have passed since the establishment of a monetary, economic and social union between the two post-war Germanys. The first stretch of the road towards integration has been difficult, straining the financial stability of western Germany and drastically reducing output and employment opportunities in the new Länder. For a better understanding of the high financial and social costs of the unification process but also for a better appreciation of the positive economic results achieved so far, it is important to bear two things in mind: first, the uniqueness of the historical and economic circumstances under which the merging of two very different economies had to be accomplished, and, second, the far-reaching implications this has had for supply and demand developments in the two parts of Germany[1]:

–   Right from the start, the economies of the new Länder were submitted to three, historically unprecedented, supply shocks. The large *de facto* revaluation of the East German mark together with the sudden full exposure to foreign and western German competition implied that large parts of the eastern German capital stock became economically unviable literally overnight. The competitive position has worsened dramatically further because of the drive towards early wage equalisation with western Germany. Although for some time to come potential output will be constrained by the availability of capital rather than labour, the medium-to-longer term output capacity will be, or has already been, reduced to the extent that the massive fall in the participation rate and the exodus of labour to western Germany proves irreversible.

–   In stark contrast, the supply potential of the western German economy has been raised as a consequence of the large intake of eastern German labour and a boost to investment in response to the creation of a larger domestic market and the expected persistence, for some years to come, of a largely government-financed eastern German supply gap.

– On the demand side, all expenditure components in the new Länder have been boosted by massive income and capital transfers from the west but there have also been three important restraining factors: eastern Germans initially repudiated their own products, trade with former CMEA countries collapsed and investment spending has been held back by unsettled property rights and administrative impediments.

– Given the lack of competitive output capacity in the new Länder, the western German economy experienced a significant demand boost from unification: apart from the above-mentioned stimulus to investment a large part of the credit-financed demand in the east has spilled over into the west. As will be discussed in more detail in the following sections, the steep increase in demand for western German goods and services has been met in several ways: increase of capacity and capacity use, massive recourse to imports and diversion of exports from traditional markets to eastern Germany, and to a limited extent also by higher prices.

1991 in retrospect: summary of annual projections and outcomes

For western Germany, the 1991 outcome for aggregate demand, output and inflation was only a little higher than projected a year ago[2]. Real GNP growth, at 3.1 per cent, remained well above its previous ten-year average of 2.4 per cent, and the GNP deflator grew less than $1/2$ percentage point faster than expected (Table 1). The biggest "surprise" was the strength of private non-residential investment, outstripping even the strong expansion of the preceding year. Total exports, which includes sales to eastern Germany, turned out less than a point faster than projected, while imports grew slightly less. The resulting greater pressure on resources was largely offset by a weakening of stockbuilding. The current external account posted a deficit much in line with the Secretariat estimate, and the general government financial deficit was somewhat lower than foreseen, reflecting an underestimation of tax revenues and some underspending on the part of the new Länder.

Table 1. **Projections and outcomes for western Germany, 1991**

Percentage changes, volume

	1990	1991 outcome	1991 OECD projection
Private consumption	4.7	2.5	2½
Public consumption	2.1	0.8	2
Gross fixed investment	8.8	6.7	5¼
Public investment	2.5	1.2	−2
Private non-residential investment	7.8	9.0	7¼
Private residential	10.5	4.1	3¼
Total domestic demand	4.5	3.0	3¼
Exports	11.0	12.1	11¼
Imports	11.6	12.6	13
GNP	4.5	3.1	2¾
Private consumption deflator	2.6	3.6	3¼
GNP deflator	3.4	4.4	4

Source: OECD, *National Accounts;* and *Economic Survey of Germany,* July 1991.

For eastern Germany a similar juxtaposition of earlier projections and out-comes cannot be presented. Firstly, because of the poor statistical basis a year ago, no quantitative projections for this region were presented in the 1991 German Survey, and secondly, full-year national accounts data for eastern Germany exist only for 1991. Half-year data have been published so far only for the second half of 1990. This means that no official basis exists for calculating year-on-year growth rates or growth rates through the year. The following review of 1991 developments will, however, draw on estimates and projections made by leading German research institutes.

Demand and output growth weakened through 1991[3]

Trends in demand

Overall demand expanded probably at only half the rate recorded for 1990. The expansion of demand in industrialised countries, in particular for capital goods, slowed down and eastern German trade with the former CMEA countries collapsed. The post-unification surge of private consumption in the new Länder seems to have petered out by mid-1991, while investment activity picked up from very depressed levels. In western Germany, total "domestic" demand was virtually flat in the second half of the year, curbed by more restrictive macroeconomic policies (see Part II).

The sharp contraction of *eastern German* GNP in 1991[4] cannot be related to lack of domestic demand: it was, as noted above, rather a lack of competitive production. The one-to-one currency conversion rate applied to contractual incomes and the steep increases in wage and non-wage labour costs during the months leading up to and following the establishment of monetary and economic union made large parts of eastern German capacity highly uncompetitive. The resulting loss of customers was exacerbated by the release of pent-up demand for western products and the collapse of demand from foreign-exchange-constrained former CMEA countries. Drastic falls of demand could only be avoided by huge transfers of financial resources from the old to the new Länder. Indeed, public-sector transfers, amounting to scme DM 120 billion, permitted the total use of resources in eastern Germany to be more than twice as much as gross national product.

After having grown rapidly in the two preceding years, the expansion of aggregate demand in the *western German* economy slowed markedly in the course of 1991. In the first half of the year, the effect of slowing world economic activity was more than offset by increased deliveries to the new Länder and continued demand strength in the old Länder. In addition, mild weather fostered activity in the first quarter. However, as the year progressed, spill-over effects from the east started to weaken, and demand in western Germany was curbed mainly by the mid-1991 tax-package, but also by continuing high interest rates (Table 2).

Table 2. **Domestic demand and GNP growth, western Germany**

Per cent change from previous period, seasonally-adjusted annual rate, volume (1985 prices)

	1990 I	1990 II	1991 I	1991 II
Total domestic demand	6.4	4.1	4.8	−0.9
GNP	6.1	4.6	4.9	−1.9

Source: OECD, *National Accounts.*

15

All-German real *private consumption* expanded in 1991 much less vigorously than in 1990, reflecting some deceleration in the growth of disposable incomes, steepening consumer price increases, and an overall rise in the household savings ratio. In the *western Länder,* continuously fast growth of employment and higher gains in earnings boosted household income before tax but in terms of disposable purchasing power there was a marked slowdown due to higher inflation and taxation: the "solidarity levy" (effective from July 1991) and the increase in social security contributions (from April 1991) together absorbed DM 23 billion, and the energy tax increase (July 1991) an additional DM 6 billion (Table 3). Even so, real disposable income continued to grow above its longer-term trend, and consumption was further supported by a tax-induced fall in the savings ratio. Less optimistic longer-term prospects for disposable income were reflected in a steep decline of consumer confidence, which started in late 1990 (Diagram 1). In *eastern Germany,* real net household incomes from gainful employment seem to have fallen slightly[5], but the loss of purchasing power was much more than offset by massive increases in transfer income[6]. However, with a progressive satisfaction of the initial pent-up demand for western consumer goods, growth of household real expenditure slowed, permitting some recovery of the savings ratio.

Table 3. **Appropriation account for households, western Germany**

Per cent changes

	1987 DM billion	1980-1989	1990	1991
Compensation of employees	1 124.7	3.9	7.5	7.9
Income from property and others	441.1	5.3	7.8	7.4
Current transfers received	412.9	4.6	4.9	6.5
less:				
Interest on consumer debt	17.5	4.4	13.4	16.4
Total income	1 931.2	4.3	6.9	7.4
less:				
Direct taxes	209.4	4.3	–3.4	18.5
Current transfers paid	454.2	4.9	6.4	7.6
Disposable income	1 267.6	4.1	9.1	5.9
Consumers' expenditure	1 108.0	4.2	7.4	6.1
Savings ratio (per cent)		12.5	13.9	13.7
Real disposable income		1.4	6.3	2.2

Source: OECD, *National Accounts.*

Diagram 1. **RETAIL TURNOVER AND CONSUMER CONFIDENCE WESTERN GERMANY**

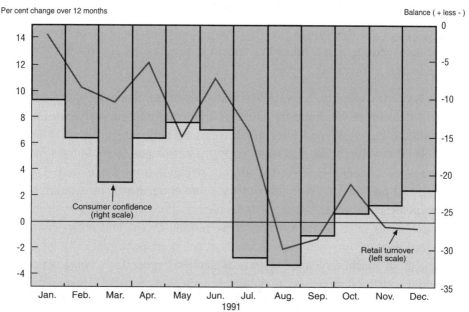

Per cent change over 12 months

Balance (+ less -)

Consumer confidence
(right scale)

Retail turnover
(left scale)

1991

Source: IFO Institute.

Fixed capital formation was the main source of demand expansion. In the *eastern Länder,* investment spending relative to final domestic resource use was only a little lower than in the western Länder (20 per cent compared with 24 per cent), though in *per capita* terms only half the western German level. Public-sector investment in infrastructure (in its broadest sense) quickly gained momentum after unification. Private investment, despite subsidisation[7], was slower to pick up. A number of measures were taken in 1991 to improve the investment climate for private investors, but investment activity continued to be hampered by:

- a deficient public infrastructure;
- unresolved property rights;
- insufficient supply of office space, construction plots and production sites, for which extremely high rents have often been asked;

17

–   an inefficient local administration in the new Länder;
huge ecological liabilities inherited from the past.

Nevertheless, total investment spending may have been about 20 per cent up on the previous year, with a third of investment in fixed assets accounted for by the private sector.

In *western Germany,* buoyant business investment demand – spurred by the sudden extension of the domestic market – continued into the early part of 1991 (Diagram 2), but weakened later in the year, probably in response to several inter-related developments: the weak export performance in traditional markets was not – as in 1990 – offset by surging demand from the eastern Länder; growing cost pressures were making inroads into companies' profits[8] and, hence, self-financing capabilities; capacity utilisation – though still high by historical standards – was falling back towards more normal levels; and prospects for an early recovery of international demand were more pessimistically assessed. Investment in machinery and equipment declined more than construction, as residential construction activity maintained much of its earlier buoyancy through the year, notwithstanding high interest rates, rising land prices and increased construction costs[9]. Despite the weakening trend during the year, the share of investment in GNP attained 22¼ per cent in 1991, the highest level since 1973, when it reached 24¼ per cent.

Growth of *public-sector consumption* decelerated rather sharply. In *western Germany,* the slower rise was to some extent a statistical artefact, as a part of federal consumption spending is treated as exports of services to the new Länder (DM 10 billion). Public consumption in the *eastern Länder* expanded only little in real terms reflecting the slimming of previously ''overstaffed'' public administrations.

Net export developments, in an accounting sense, acted as a strong drag on total production growth in 1991. In the *eastern Länder,* exports plummeted, notably in the first half of the year, being on average 40 per cent below the 1990 level. Virtually the entire decline occurred in trade with the former Soviet Union and other former CMEA countries. In contrast, *western German* export volumes, which include deliveries to the eastern Länder, posted a steep 12 per cent increase. However, apart from these deliveries, real exports expanded only very little (Table 4). In fact, German commodity exports have been stagnating since

18

Diagram 2. **INVESTMENT SPENDING, WESTERN GERMANY**

Index 1989 = 100

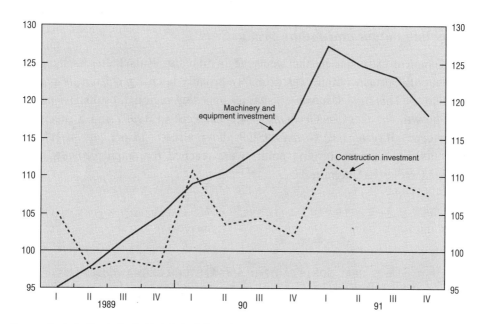

Source: Deutsche Bundesbank, *Statistische Beihefte,* Reihe 4.

mid-1990, reflecting both weak international demand, notably for capital goods, where German firms tend to be specialised[10], and stiffer competition from foreign firms facing declining capacity utilisation[11]. With a continued high "pass-

Table 4. **Change in real net goods and services exports, western Germany**

In per cent of GNP, change from previous year

	1990 I	1990 II	1991 I	1991 II
Total	−1.1	+1.3	+0.9	−0.5
Eastern Germany	+0.7	+5.3	+6.7	+2.3
Foreign countries	−1.8	−4.0	−5.8	−2.8

Source: Deutsche Bundesbank.

19

through'' of eastern German import demand, western German import volumes grew strongly (13 per cent), despite declining capacity utilisation.

Stagnating output and falling productivity

Tentative estimates by the Deutsche Institut für Wirtschaftsforschung suggest that all-German output was probably broadly unchanged from its previous year's level. This masks, however, sharply opposing regional results: 3.4 per cent GDP growth for *western Germany*[12] (4.7 per cent in 1990) and a precipitous 34 per cent fall of *eastern German* GDP (down already 15 per cent in 1990). In the course of the year, turning points were reached for output growth in both parts of Germany (Diagram 3):

Diagram 3. **REAL GDP IN EASTERN AND WESTERN GERMANY, 1989-1991**
Index 1989 = 100

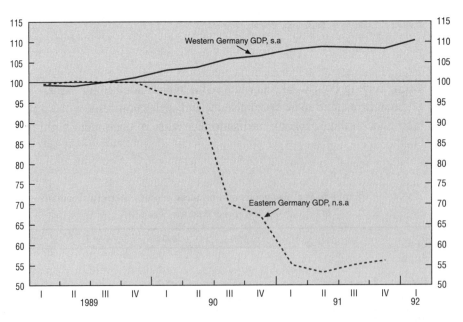

Source: Deutsche Bundesbank, *Statistische Beihefte, Reihe 4,* and Ifo-Institute.

- After a steep increase in the first two quarters of 1991, *western German* real GDP declined during the remainder of the year. The slower rise in output was mainly felt on labour productivity growth: after having increased 1¾ per cent in 1990, output per person employed rose only ¾ per cent, while employment grew 2½ per cent (3 per cent in 1990)[13].
- The output contraction in the *eastern Länder* came to an end by mid-1991, with a highly differentiated picture between different subsectors of the economy: manufacturing production was fairly flat in the course of the year, while strong increases were recorded in trade, services and construction. Productivity developments are difficult to gauge for the *eastern Länder,* as large-scale employment-support schemes have blurred the distinction between active and non-active labour. While those employed are becoming more productive, there is still some "labour-hoarding" in Treuhandanstalt firms and "employment companies". As a result, measured aggregate output per person employed may have fallen by as much as 20 per cent in 1991, and even allowing for cuts in average annual work hours, there would still seem to have been some decline in hourly productivity. Hence, as shown in Table 5, the relative size of the economy shrank further (from just over to just below 7 per cent of the total) and eastern German GDP per employee was less than 30 per cent of that of western Germany, while average monthly salaries in the eastern Länder had already reached 45 per cent of the western German level (see below).

Table 5. **Comparative statistics: eastern and western Germany, 1991**

DM

	Eastern Germany	Western Germany	Ratio (east/west) per cent
GNP (billion)	193	2 615	7.3
GNP per capita	12 000	41 000	29.2
GDP per employee[1]	25 500	89 100	28.6
Average monthly salaries[1]	1 850	3 980	46.5

1. Domestic basis – i.e. based on place of work, not residence.
Source: Statistisches Bundesamt, *Volkswirtschaftliche Gesamtrechnungen,* Fachserie 18.

The labour market: falling unemployment in the west – falling employment in the east

Since 1989, job creation in western Germany has been much stronger than in the preceding decade: employment has risen by about 2 million, roughly corresponding to the number of unemployed in 1988 (Table 6). However, as the supply of labour increased by about 1½ million, the decline in unemployment was limited to about ½ million. Roughly 60 per cent of the additional demand for labour appears to have been satisfied from the pool of "new" Germans (ethnic Germans, migrants and commuters from eastern Germany)[14]; 25 per cent through a reflow out of unemployed; while the rest was made up from foreign workers[15]. In 1991, total employment increased by 2½ per cent to 29¼ million people. Dependent employment increased faster (2¾ per cent), while self-employment rose more slowly. The number of short-time workers rose but unemployment

Table 6. **The western German labour market**

	1989	1990	1991
	Change in 1 000 to previous year		
Supply	160	670	776
Germans	79	493	520
Demographic change	−35	−96	−133
Migrants and immigrants	68	359	324
Pendler, net	39	145	289
Residual	−7	85	40
Guest workers and asylum seekers	81	177	256
Demand	370	802	804
Germans	281	681	710
Foreign workers	89	121	94
Registered unemployed	−204	−155	−194
'Quiet" reserve[1]	−6	23	166
Germans	−35	−63	9
Foreign workers	29	86	157
Unemployment rate[2]	7.9	7.2	6.3

1. The "quiet" reserve includes asylum seekers who are not registered as unemployed, but also "discouraged" workers. As of July 1991, asylum seekers who had to wait for five years to get a working permit before, have immediate access to the labour market.
2. As a percentage of the dependent labour force.
Source: Bach H-U., *et al.,* 1991, "Der Arbeitsmarkt in der Bundesrepublik Deutschland 1991/92", *Mitteilungen aus der Arbeitsmarkt- und Berufsforschung,* 4/91.

Table 7. **The labour market in the eastern Länder**

	1990	1991
	Change in 1 000 to previous year	
Supply	−787	−947
Pendler, net	−68	−289
Migration, net	−359	−173
Early retirement	−180	−220
Pre-retiring	−10	−179
Training	−5	−115
Residual	−165	29
Demand	−1 027	−1 620
Full-time employment	−1 406	−2 146
Employment companies	0	250
Short-time work[1]	379	526
Registered unemployed	240	673

1. Full-time equivalent.
Source: Buttler F., 1991, "Der Arbeitsmarkt in den neuen Bundesländern 1991/92", *Mitteilungen aus der Arbeitsmarkt- und Berufsforschung,* 4/91.

declined for the third consecutive year: at 1.7 million people, it was more than 600 000 lower than at the peak years 1985 to 1988, and the lowest for more than a decade.

The unusually fast employment growth experienced over the past few years has been fostered by the steeply rising inflow of ethnic Germans and *Pendler.* The high absorption capacity of the labour market, which contrasts with the experience during the 1980s, may reflect several factors specific for the new additions to the labour force and different from the profile of the typical unemployed worker in western Germany: the reservation wage for the new supply of labour was lower (complaints were voiced about so-called "wage-dumping", notably in the construction sector); and motivation was high, as was occupational and regional mobility. Finally, skills and age structures seem to have matched better the existing stock of vacancies[16].

With production collapsing in *eastern Germany* since unification, labour shedding has taken considerable proportions: while at mid-1990 there were over 9 million[17] in work, there were about 6¾ million employed by the end of 1991 (excluding *Pendler*). This decline in employment was not reflected one-to-one in registered unemployment: while about 2½ million jobs were lost, the labour supply simultaneously shrunk by 1¾ million, leaving just under 1 million persons unemployed on average for 1991. The path of both labour demand and supply was significantly influenced by a massive deployment of labour-market measures, subsidies to employment, and other measures of (temporary) employment protection and support to output (for details see Part IV).

On commuters or *Pendler* from the eastern Länder

The *western German* labour market attracted up to end 1991 more than 500 000 commuters, or, to use the German word, *Pendler* from the eastern Länder. The *Pendler* are typically young (on average 31, compared to a western German average of 38) and skilled (69 per cent) blue-collar workers. However, only 51 per cent have a job in their own profession probably due to a downgrading of occupational levels. As to the sectoral distribution of this new employment, more than 25 per cent found a job in manufacturing; 15 per cent in trade, 13 per cent in construction and services, respectively; 10 per cent found a job in transport, and the rest are in other sectors.

Most *Pendler* have sought employment in former "depressed" regions with high unemployment rates (over 30 per cent work in Berlin-West, most others work along the former border area). The mobility of *Pendler* is high: the average daily commuting distance is 50 kilometres and 44 per cent commute weekly or at longer intervals.

Survey results suggest that *Pendler* almost doubled their income. Nevertheless, only 50 per cent indicated that the income gain was the main incentive for commuting. Despite the rapid catch-up with western wage levels in eastern Germany, the number of commuters more than doubled during 1991, suggesting that "push" factors – namely joblessness – has become more relevant for the decision to seek employment "on the other side". On the other hand, some 40 per cent of the *Pendler* expressed a clear preference for staying in the eastern Länder[18].

An intensifying cost-price spiral

In 1991, price and cost developments moved further away from the objective of price stability, though for partly different reasons in the two parts of Germany. In the eastern Länder, where the consumer price index in December was 21 per cent up on the year earlier, price developments have been strongly influenced by ongoing adjustments of highly subsidised prices to free market levels: year-on-year increases for transport tariffs were 11 per cent, for energy prices 236 per cent and for car insurance, postal charges and rents 309 per cent. In contrast, industrial producer prices remained virtually stable. At the same time, cost pressures have intensified: the weak state of the labour market notwithstanding, gross earnings increased by some 65 per cent between April 1990 and the third quarter 1991. The catching-up with western German wages has been most pronounced in the construction sector where by October 1991, average monthly wages and salaries attained 65 per cent of the western German level (up from 44 per cent in July 1990), while for manufacturing the relative wage levels clustered around the 45 per cent mark.

In the western Länder, prices were raised by fiscal measures but otherwise driven by cost inflation (Diagram 4):

-   Reflecting high 1991 wage settlements ranging between 6 and 7½ per cent, increases in social security contributions and sluggish productivity

Diagram 4. **COST AND PRICE DEVELOPMENTS, WESTERN GERMANY**

Per cent increase over a year earlier

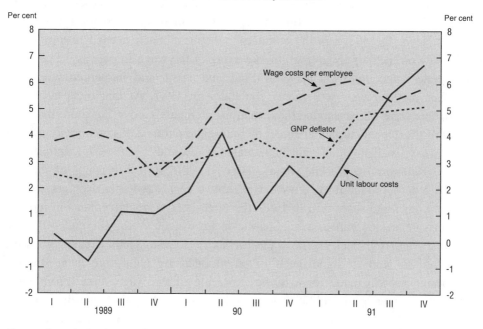

Source: Deutsche Bundesbank, Statistische Beihefte, Reihe 4.

advances, year-on-year unit labour cost increases more than doubled between the two halves of the year (from less than $3\frac{1}{2}$ to $6\frac{1}{2}$ per cent).

– Excise taxes, notably on energy products, were increased (on average by 25 per cent), as of mid-year.

– While fiercer international competition kept the twelve-month rate of producer price increases at around $2\frac{1}{2}$ per cent until the end of the year (with export price increases below $1\frac{1}{2}$ per cent), the ability to pass higher costs on to prices remained quite strong in more domestically-oriented sectors, notably construction and services.

– Although in the course of 1991 import prices dropped below their corresponding previous year's level, the twelve-month growth rate of the cost-of-living index accelerated from 2.7 per cent in the first quarter to almost 4 per cent in the fourth quarter. Over the same period, the underlying rise in prices, as measured by quarter-to-quarter changes in the non-food, non-energy component of the consumer price index, picked up from about $\frac{1}{2}$ per cent to over $1\frac{1}{4}$ per cent.

The recent acceleration of wages is partly a reaction to the decline in the share of wages in national income in the 1980s, which bottomed out in 1990 at its lowest level for 30 years the counterpart being a much needed restoration of adequate profit margins. In part, the lowering of the wage-share was the result of moderate wage contracts between 1983 and 1989, and in particular a large number of three-year settlements concluded in 1987. At that time, economic prospects were rather subdued and many settlements – covering more than one third of the dependent labour force, including the public sector – were agreed for three years with nominal annual increases of around 3 per cent, together with some reductions in working hours. However, the strong upswing of the late 1980s led to productivity growth well above real wage increases and consequently the wage share fell. In 1990, the three-year wage agreements in most of the private sector ended, while public-sector wages were still under the old contracts and fell back in the wage hierarchy. Private sector settlements were expected to lead to some catch-up on productivity gains, but even stronger economic growth made for a further lowering of the wage share. From January 1991, wages in the public sector rose by 6 per cent, again lower than in most private sector industries. With strong employment growth the share of wages in national income rose in 1991, regaining the level of the mid-1980s.

Turnaround of the current external account

The decline in national saving – reflecting credit-financed increases in public transfers – and the simultaneous rise in the all-German investment ratio shifted the current account of the balance of payments from substantial surplus to a moderate deficit: from a surplus of $47 billion (DM 76 billion or 3 per cent of GNP) in 1990 to a deficit of $20 billion (DM 33 billion or 1¼ per cent of GNP) in 1991. With overall cost competitiveness improving somewhat in 1991, the major factors behind the swing were faster 'growth of domestic demand in Germany than in major trading partner countries, trade diversion to expand supply in the eastern German market and significantly higher official transfers to abroad.

Table 8. **Exports and competitiveness**

Per cent changes, 1985 prices

	1988	1989	1990	1991
Total exports	6.3	10.2	5.4	1.5
of which:				
Goods	6.4	7.9	1.5	−2.3
Services	−2.1	10.5	2.1	0.2
Manufacturing exports				
Volume growth	7.4	8.2	1.2	−4.0
Market growth	9.3	8.7	5.3	1.3
Export performance	−1.7	−0.5	−3.9	−5.2
Export prices	0.9	4.3	−0.7	0.1
Relative export prices	−2.9	−1.7	4.1	−1.2
Relative unit labour costs	0.0	−3.9	3.1	−1.7
Memorandum item:				
World trade [1]	8.5	6.8	5.3	3.9

1. Arithmetic average of world import and export volumes.
Source: OECD.

German manufacturing exports slumped in 1991, reflecting both the diversion of western German sales from traditional foreign markets towards eastern Germany and the collapse of eastern German trade with the former CMEA countries. Hence with foreign markets growing, though at diminishing rates, there was a continuing loss of market shares (Table 8). On the import side, strong increases were recorded in line with overall demand growth. A worsening of the terms of trade (by 1 ½ per cent) also contributed to the marked slimming of the overall trade surplus (from DM 105 billion to DM 22 billion) (Table 9). European Community countries "benefited" most, their deficit vis-à-vis Germany being reduced from DM 64 billion to DM 25 billion. The surplus in the bilateral trade with the United States disappeared and the deficit against Japan widened further.

Table 9. **Components of the current account of the balance of payments**

DM billion

	1990	1991
Exports of goods (fob)	662.0	665.8
Imports of goods (cif)	556.7	649.9
Trade balance	105.4	21.9
Services:		
Investment income, net	27.6	29.0
Travel, net	−30.4	−33.4
Receipts of foreign military agencies	21.1	21.4
Other service transactions	−10.9	−12.6
Balance on services	7.4	4.4
Net contribution to EC	−11.0	−18.4
Other official transfers	−14.4	−29.4
Private transfers	−11.3	−11.4
Balance on transfers	−36.7	−59.1
Current account	76.1	−32.9
Per cent of GNP	3.1	−1.2
Memorandum items:		
Trade balance against EC countries	64.2	24.8
Trade balance against the United States	9.9	−1.3
Trade balance against Japan	−15.5	−23.2

Source: Deutsche Bundesbank.

The surplus on the service balance was virtually eliminated, mainly due to a rapidly rising deficit on tourism. Net investment income, a major contributor to service earnings, rose only moderately as returns on financial investments fell.

Higher EC contributions, the first instalments of agreed payments for Soviet troop withdrawals (DM 2½ billion) and Gulf War contributions (DM 12 billion), led to a near doubling of official transfers to about DM 48 billion in 1991 and a rise of total net transfers from almost DM 37 billion in 1990 to DM 59 billion.

Table 10. **The capital account**

	1989	1990	1991
Long-term capital			
Direct investment	−14.2	−33.3	−30.9
Securities	−5.0	−6.4	37.7
Bank loans	13.0	−20.0	−27.8
Official loans	−9.4	−6.7	−3.5
Other	−7.0	0.1	−3.3
Balance	−22.5	−66.2	−27.9
Short-term capital			
Banks	−56.7	0.6	39.8
Enterprises	−51.6	−19.4	7.1
Official	−4.8	−5.2	−4.7
Balance	−113.1	−23.9	42.3
Balance on capital account	−135.6	−90.1	14.4
Balance of unclassifiable transactions	8.6	25.0	18.8
Change in net external assets of the Bundesbank	−21.6	5.9	0.8

Source: Deutsche Bundesbank.

Although the shift in the current external position was large, over 4 per cent of GNP, the corresponding redirection of capital flows took place without difficulty (Table 10). Having been a large net capital exporter (DM 90 billion in 1990 or 3 per cent of GNP), Germany has become a net capital importer of some size: in 1991 the net inflow attained DM 14 billion (½ per cent of GNP). The larger part of the financing took the form of short term capital imports as both banks and enterprises took advantage of lower borrowing costs abroad. Net long-term capital exports were more than halved compared to 1990 (DM 28 billion against DM 66 billion), reflecting in particular increased foreign investments in government paper. The net outflow of direct investment was only little affected by unification.

II. Efforts to safeguard macroeconomic stability

Since unification, all aspects of economic policy – fiscal, monetary and structural – have been under increasingly intensive pressure. This reflects not only the weaker conjunctural situation since mid-1991, surveyed in Part I, and the underestimation of the shocks to which the new Länder have been exposed, but also the fact that policy choices had to be made and numerous programmes to be put together at considerable speed. This has introduced inefficiencies and distortions into the emerging markets and has incurred significant deadweight losses.

Fiscal policy: striving to contain borrowing requirements

As the poor state of the former GDR economy was progressively revealed, it became clear that the massive task of integrating the eastern German economy could not be accomplished without imposing substantial burdens on the western German economy. The inevitable initial phase of ''creative destruction'' could be managed neither politically nor socially without substantial material assistance:

- financial provision had to be made to help establish and man the new public institutions at the Länder and municipal level;
- the public infrastructure had to be modernised and extended;
- the attractiveness of the new Länder for investment and production had to be promoted;
- income and capital transfers had to be used to narrow the huge gap between the potential level of ''warranted'', (that is, market-generated) incomes, and the aspirations of the eastern German population, inspired by agreements embodied in the State and Unification Treaties as well as by political announcements.

1991: higher spending pressure met with higher taxation

Following a series of *ad hoc* emergency measures in the course of 1990 and the subsequent adoption of three supplementary budgets, there was great uncertainty about the size of future financial requirements and their mode of financing. The 1991 federal budget, voted in February 1991, incorporated aid to the east of some DM 75 billion; social contributions had already been raised with effect from 1 April, raising DM 12 billion in the first year. Additional support for the east was provided in March through the "Upswing East" programme. Worth DM 24 billion and covering two years, it was primarily designed to strengthen investment on a broad scale. Subsequently, faced with steeply-rising international commitments – higher EC payments, increased aid to Eastern Europe, the first payments for the withdrawal of former USSR troops from the new Länder, and Gulf War contributions – it became clear that these extra efforts could not be wholly financed within planned recourse to the capital market. Hence, with effect from 1 July 1991:

- income taxes were raised for twelve months via an additional 7½ per cent levy on income tax liabilities ("the solidarity levy"), boosting 1991 tax revenues by DM 10½ billion;
- indirect taxes were increased on mineral oil (on average 25 per cent) and on insurance (from 7 per cent to 10 per cent) with an estimated revenue effect for 1991 of some DM 7 billion.

The impact on public finances of the first eighteen months of economic unification has been fairly dramatic, causing a sharp reversal of past trends (Diagram 5): the rise in general government spending in 1990 and 1991 relative to GNP has wiped out virtually all consolidation gains obtained in the years 1982-89. At the same time the rise in taxation and social security contributions in 1991 has brought the tax burden back to the level prior to the 1986-90 Tax Reform Programme.

Better-than-expected outcomes for 1991

In 1991, the all-German general government deficit on a national-accounts basis[19], though at DM 77 billion two-thirds higher than in 1990, turned out to be markedly lower than expected earlier (Table 11). High spending increases were recorded for the wage and salary bill, transfers to households and firms and on

Diagram 5.

Diagram 5. **TREND IN GENERAL GOVERNMENT SPENDING, TAXATION AND FINANCIAL BALANCE**

Per cent of GNP

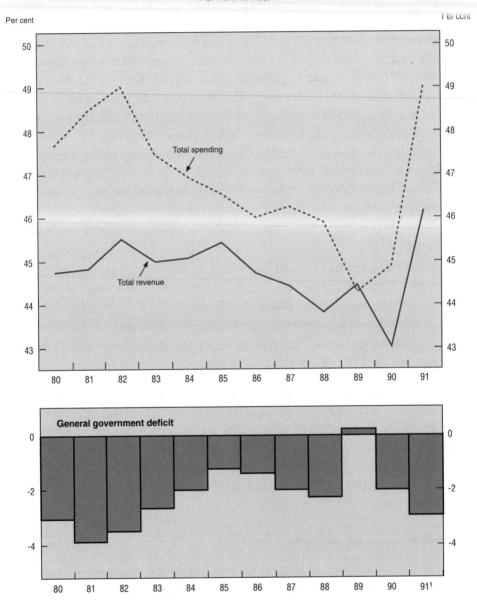

1. In per cent of all German GNP.
Source: OECD.

32

Table 11. **General government appropriation account**

DM billion

	1987	1988	1989	1990[1]	1991[2]
Revenue					
Taxes	489.5	509.5	558.0	571.3	687.4
Social security contributions	350.6	366.0	382.8	408.6	510.5
Other revenue	51.3	48.9	58.1	61.1	73.7
Total	841.4	924.2	998.9	1 041.0	1 271.6
Outlays					
Consumption	397.3	412.4	418.9	447.3	559.8
Subsidies	44.8	47.7	45.4	46.7	63.7
Social security	328.2	343.2	358.4	374.0	475.8
Other transfers	41.8	47.5	47.6	94.6	77.9
Interest payments	57.8	59.9	60.4	64.2	77.3
Investment	48.0	48.9	52.7	56.7	72.2
Other outlays[3]	11.4	10.1	10.1	5.8	22.2
Total	929.3	969.7	993.5	1 089.3	1 348.9
Net lending	–37.9	–45.3	5.4	–48.3	–77.3
As per cent of GNP	–1.9	–2.2	0.2	–2.0	2.8[4]
Memorandum items (DM billion):					
Net lending of:					
Central government[5]	–28.2	–34.6	–9.6	–53.1	–77.8
Länder government	–16.6	–14.9	–4.7	–14.0	n.a.
Communes	0.2	2.6	2.7	–1.5	n.a.
Social security	6.6	1.6	17.0	20.3	20.4

1. As from the second half of 1990, including transfers to eastern Germany and the budget deficit of the GDR government. Preliminary data.
2. Including Länder and Municipalities in eastern Germany.
3. Including net capital transfers.
4. As a per cent of all-German GNP.
5. Including Unity fund and debt management fund.
Source: OECD, *National Accounts;* Ministry of Finance.

investment. Revenues were boosted by the tax measures mentioned above but also by the high 1991 wage settlements and continued buoyancy of consumer demand.

The better-than-expected outcome was mainly attributable to the lower *federal government* deficit (DM 8.6 billion less than budgeted), reflecting less spending, notably on transfers to the Labour Office and the Debt-management fund (Kreditabwicklungsfonds)[20] but also faster rising tax revenues. Apart from higher international commitments, additional federal government spending

33

mainly arose from unification. Indeed, about a fifth of total expenditure was directly related to the unification process, a third of which provided social flanking to the reconstruction process in the eastern Länder (for details see below). The ensuing need for expenditure restraint in other areas was partly met by one-off cuts in defence appropriations, redirection of investment spending to the east and by cyclically-induced underspending on labour-market measures in western Germany. Some budget relief was obtained from subsidy reductions (see below).

Spending by the western Länder and Municipalities, though carrying only a small proportion of the unification costs, increased by 7 and 9 per cent, respectively, driven, in particular, by personnel outlays and interest payments. Pressure on public expenditure was also strong in the eastern Länder: per capita outlays reached 90 per cent of the western level, mainly reflecting high transfer payments to households (subsidies for heating, transport and rents), subsidies to firms and personnel expenditure, the latter attaining 81 per cent of the western per capita level[21].

Higher public sector deficit in prospect for 1992

On current plans the *general government* deficit will increase further in 1992, reaching DM 90 billion or 3 per cent of GNP. Revenues will be boosted by continuing strong growth in taxable incomes, higher Bundesbank profits, and the full-year effect of last year's indirect tax increases. On the other hand, the solidarity surcharge on income taxes will end in-mid year and contributions to the unemployment insurance have been lowered. Overall spending is set to rise vigorously, despite the relief from outlays associated with the Gulf war. Net transfers to the eastern Länder will rise and, following a Constitutional Court ruling, family tax allowances and benefits are to be significantly improved. With the western German pension law being extended to eastern Germany, and more massive deployment of labour market measures, the social security sector may post a deficit of some DM 11 billion in 1992, after having been in a surplus of DM 20 billion in 1991 owing to strong employment growth in western Germany since 1988.

The 1992 Federal budget, including the May supplementary budget, with a financial deficit of around DM 41 billion (Table 12) is set to reduce further the federal share in the overall public-sector deficit. Relatively fast spending growth

Table 12. **The federal budget**

DM billion

	1989	1990[1]	1991 Proposed	1991 Outcome	1992 Proposed[2]
Expenditure	289.8	380.2	410.3	401.8	425.1
of which:					
Consumption expenditures	82.2	85.6	97.0	91.8	97.5
Interest payments	32.1	34.2	42.5	39.6	44.3
Investment	8.0	8.5	11.5	11.0	14.1
Transfers to other					
administrations	37.2	41.5	67.2	65.7	78.5
Other	130.3	210.5	192.1	193.7	190.7
Revenues	269.7	332.1	348.7	348.6	383.7
of which:					
Taxes	247.1	276.0	316.5	317.9	350.2
Other income	22.6	56.0	32.2	30.7	33.5
Financial balance	–20.1	–48.0	–61.7	–53.2	–41.0
As per cent of GNP	–0.9	–2.0	–2.2	–1.9	–1.4

1. Including 1st to 3rd supplementary budget, the latter incorporating the GDR budget for the second half of 1990.
2. Including first supplementary budget.
Source: Submissions from the Ministry of Finance and the *Finanzplan 1990* and *Finanzplan 1991*.

– more than 5 per cent – must be seen against the backdrop of recorded underspending in the eastern Länder in 1991, which now seems to be coming to an end[22]. Appropriations for unification-related outlays are markedly higher than in 1991 (DM 110 billion against DM 90 billion). Being fully financed out of the extra revenue from the solidarity levy, they cover the second tranche of the "Upswing East"-programme (DM 12 billion), which shifts the emphasis from municipal investment grants and one-off payments to wider infrastructure investment.

Rising public transfers to the new Länder

As noted above, the financial burden on the public sector associated with the reconstruction of the economy of the eastern Länder has proved to be much larger than initially expected. More and more resources were made available for job-preserving and job-creating measures and for the support of the unemployed.

In addition, the state of the eastern infrastructure has proved to be much worse than thought prior to unification. The weaker starting base of viable production and for gainful employment also meant weak tax revenues. Indeed, the eastern Länder, with a population share of 20 per cent, are estimated to have provided some 6 per cent of total all-German public-sector tax revenues in 1991.

Public gross financial resources to be made available for the eastern Länder are estimated to reach DM 218 billion in 1992, up from DM 170 billion in 1991[23]; this corresponds to 6½ and 5½ per cent of GNP, respectively. Adjusted for federal taxes and social security contributions, the net transfer may amount to DM 180 billion (DM 139 billion in 1991)[24]. Diagram 6 gives the main sources and uses of gross transfers. The largest contributor is the federal government with a 50 per cent share (including some expenditure directed through the Unity Fund), with the social security system providing some 20 per cent and the Unity and other funds most of the remainder.

Within the social security system it is the unemployment and (more recently) the pension insurance schemes that have been financially most burdened by unification. With the steep increase in unemployment and the massive deployment of labour market measures, the net transfer from the Labour Office to the eastern Länder amounted to about DM 25 billion in 1991 and for 1992 a transfer of DM 30 billion is expected. With the extension of the western German pension legislation to the eastern Länder, a transfer of DM 15 billion is likely to occur in 1992.

The Unity Fund was created to finance the deficits of the new Länder and Municipalities, with total borrowing limited to DM 95 billion for the years 1990 to 1994 and an additional DM 20 billion provided by the federal government. Resources for the Fund have been increased by more than DM 30 billion from 1993, bringing its total financing capacity up to DM 146 billion (Table 13). The additional transfers will be financed out of higher VAT revenue as from 1993[25].

The ERP special fund and the specialised federal credit institutes, i.e. the Kreditanstalt für Wiederaufbau and the Deutsche Ausgleichsbank, grant and subsidise credits for small and medium-sized enterprises, for housing, and for municipal infrastructure investments. By the end of 1991, preferential credits had been extended to the tune of DM 20 billion.

Diagram 6. **SOURCES AND USES OF TRANSFERS TO THE EASTERN LÄNDER 1992**

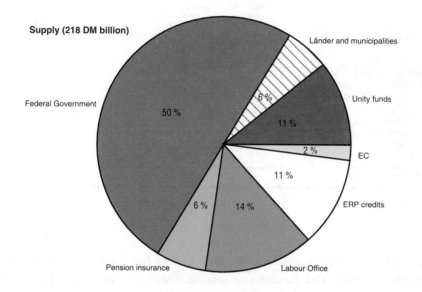

Supply (218 DM billion)

Länder and municipalities

Federal Government

50 %

6 %

Unity funds

11 %

2 % EC

11 %

ERP credits

6 % 14 %

Pension insurance

Labour Office

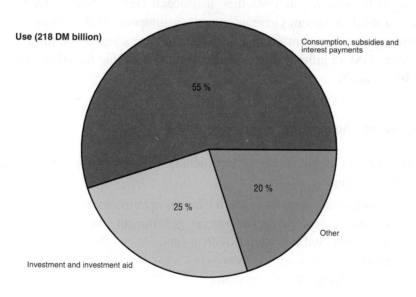

Use (218 DM billion)

Consumption, subsidies and interest payments

55 %

20 %

25 %

Other

Investment and investment aid

Source: Deutsche Bundesbank.

Table 13. **The Unity Fund**

DM billion

	1990	1991	1992	1993	1994
Lending capacity Financing	22.0	35.0	33.9	31.5	23.9
of which:					
The bond market	20.0	31.0	24.0	15.0	5.0
Federal government	2.0	4.0	9.9	12.6	14.1
of which:					
Savings on German division	2.0	4.0	4.0	5.0	5.0
From the 1993 VAT increase	–	–	–	6.6	8.1
Other	–	–	5.9	1.0	1.0
Länder	–	–	–	3.9	4.8

Source: Ministry of Finance.

About half of total transfers to the new Länder has been absorbed for non-investment purposes. The largest part of these was accounted for by current transfers to households: in 1992 they may reach DM 85 billion, financing as much as a third of eastern German private consumption. DM 55 billion are for investment and investment promotion, either for financing public infrastructure investment (DM 15 billion) or providing subsidised lending for private investors (DM 40 billion)[26].

Public sector borrowing requirement

The state of public finances is officially monitored using two different statistical recordings:

- the *net credit demand of the territorial authorities* on a financial statistics basis, comprising the federal government, the Länder and local authorities, and the various federal funds[27];
- *general government net borrowing,* covering the territorial authorities and the social security system.

The main difference between the two concepts, apart from the institutional coverage, is that the former is measured on an administrative basis and includes

38

purely financial transactions, counting government loans as expenditure and drawings on reserves as receipts, while the latter (on a national accounts basis) measures the change in the government's net wealth position. Over the last decade, the difference between the general government financial balance on national-accounts and financial-statistics basis has varied between DM 8 and 24 billion, with the surpluses on the latter invariably being smaller or deficits higher than on the former. Between half and two-thirds of this difference is attributable to the inclusion of financial transactions above the line, while the rest reflects timing adjustments.

Table 14.   **Components of public-sector financial balance**

DM billion

	1989	1990	1991	1992
Administrative basis				
Financial balances				
Federal government	−20.1	−48.0	−53.2	−41.0
State and local government, western Germany	−5.5	−23.6	−22.0	−16.5
State and local government, eastern Germany	–	–	11.0	−19.0
Unity fund	–	−20.0	−31.0	−24.0
Other funds	−1.2	−2.0	−6.0	−10.5
Territorial authorities	−26.8	−93.6	−122.0	−111.0
Social security	15.3	18.1	20.4	−11.4
Public authorities	−11.5	−75.5	−101.6	−122.4
National accounts basis				
Financial transactions and timing adjustment	15.7	29.3	24.3	32.4
General government financial balance	4.2	−46.2	−77.3	−90.0
Per cent of GNP[1]	0.2	−1.9	−2.8	−3.0
Memorandum items:				
Borrowing requirement				
Treuhandanstalt	–	9.0	10.0	30.0
Bundespost, Bundesbahn and Reichsbahn	10.0	10.0	10.0	20.0

1. From 1991 as per cent of all-German GNP.
Source: Ministry of Finance.

The choice of the relevant concept depends on the problem to be analysed: in assessing the effects on income and spending in the economy or changes in public sector net debt, the national-accounts definition is the most appropriate, if the problem at hand is to evaluate effects of public sector transactions for financial markets, the administrative basis may be more useful. Based on official estimates and projections for 1991 and 1992, the following picture emerges with respect to the above two institutional and definitional categorisations (Table 14).

- the net credit demand of the territorial authorities, estimated at DM 122 billion in 1991, is expected to decline to DM 112 billion in 1992;
- general government net borrowing may rise from DM 77 billion in 1991 to DM 90 billion in 1992;

Unification has significantly increased the public sector recourse to the German capital market: a considerable part of aggregate private savings, mostly originating from western Germany, has been used to finance the cost of social flanking and reconstruction of the new Länder. As noted above, this has had and will continue to have consequences for Germany's position as a net absorber of or supplier to world savings. In order to gain a full picture of current and future claims on the German capital market arising from activities related to the public sector and public enterprises in the context of the unification process, the borrowing by the Treuhandanstalt and extra credit demand of the eastern German Reichsbahn, the Bundesbahn and the Bundespost have to be considered together with public sector borrowing requirements.

The Treuhandanstalt's borrowing mostly finances current operations. It is treated as part of business-sector borrowing. Once the Treuhandanstalt is wound up, its accumulated debt will become the responsibility of the Federal and the Länder governments. As can be seen from Table 14 Treuhand borrowing is expected to attain DM 30 billion this year, up from DM 10 billion in 1991. It is very uncertain how much of this can be financed later by privatisation of industrial and real estate property. Capital market activities of public enterprises' are closer to those of the private sector. With part of their spending directly financed by transfers already included in the federal budget, Reichsbahn, Bundesbahn and Bundespost credits are mainly raised for investment purposes to improve the infrastructure in the eastern Länder. Since unification, credit demands of these enterprises have doubled from about DM 10 to 20 billion.

Medium-term fiscal consolidation

After having willy-nilly permitted the 1982-1989 budget consolidation process to go into reverse in the years 1990 to 1992, the Government seems firmly determined to reduce the deficit of the territorial authorities from its present annual level of about DM 125 billion to DM 78 billion by 1995. For the Federal Government this has been explicitly formalised in the latest medium-term financial plan, which by limiting federal spending growth to just 2¼ per cent per annum, provides for a deficit of just DM 25 billion in 1995 (from DM 53 billion in 1991) (Table 15). The medium-term plan also incorporates a reduction of subsidies (grants and tax allowances) by a cumulative DM 30 billion by 1994 relative to baseline. However, as noted in last year's Survey of Germany[28], the final results of such plans depend crucially on developments in the eastern Länder, which are much more difficult to project than those for western Germany. A sustained upswing in the east would in itself greatly help pave the way for a deficit reduction, while in the case of major delays in the catch-up process, high or perhaps even rising claims on financial resources might have to

Table 15. **The federal government medium-term financial plan**
DM billion

	1991	1992	1993	1994	1995[1]	1996
Outlays	413.9	425.1	435.7	452.0	452.0	465.0
of which:						
Personnel	50.7	51.3	54.6	57.4	59.3	n.a.
Services in kind	46.2	45.8	44.8	43.8	43.0	n.a.
Interest payments	42.5	44.7	51.3	55.6	59.8	n.a.
Investments	11.5	14.1	14.6	15.3	16.7	n.a.
Revenue	351.2	384.6	397.7	423.0	427.0	445.0
Financial balance	−62.6	−40.5	−38.0	−29.0	−25.0	−20.0

1. Including the expected effects of the revised *Finanzausgleich* system which will reduce both outlays and revenue.
Source: Ministry of Finance, *Finanzplan* 1992 to 1996, as of July 1992; breakdown of outlays as of August 1991.

Diagram 7. **PUBLIC SECTOR INDEBTEDNESS**

DM billion

DM billion

- Housing debt
- Treuhandanstalt
- Debt management fund
- Unity fund
- Territorial authorities

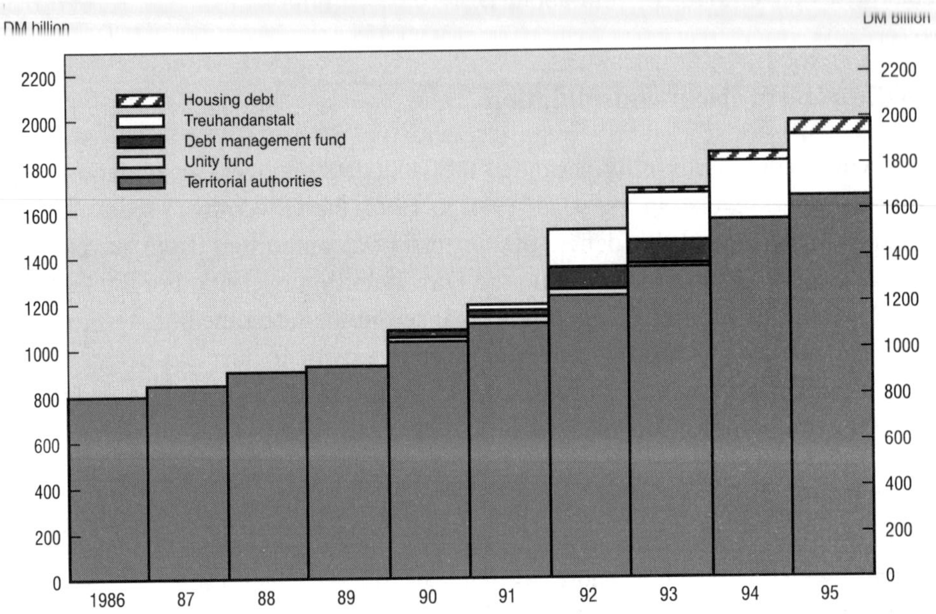

Sources: Deutsche Bundesbank and Ministry of Finance.

be met for a longer period. Other uncertainties relate to future costs of borrowing and the rate of growth of the western German economy.

Estimates of public-sector indebtedness to be reached by the middle of this decade (Diagram 7) allow rough quantitative estimates to be made about the degree of budget consolidation needed over the coming three years to meet the medium-term objectives:

- indebtedness of the territorial authorities may reach DM 1 600 billion or 45 per cent of GNP by 1995 with the associated interest payments attaining DM 125 billion;
- including the debt of the Treuhandanstalt (DM 250 billion in 1995) and the commitment to take over old debt in the eastern German housing stock (DM 62 billion) – the level of public-sector indebtedness would

42

increase to DM 1 900 billion (50 per cent of GNP). Debt servicing would be about DM 150 billion.

Scaling back the overall deficit of the territorial authorities to meet the DM 80 billion target in 1995 would require a primary surplus of about DM 30 to 40 billion to be built-up within three years. Hence, with an estimated primary deficit for 1992 of some DM 30 billion, the necessary swing would have to be DM 60 to 70 billion.

Such a consolidation path will require a high degree of spending restraint on all levels of government, leaving no room for slippage in relation to the 3 per cent guideline for territorial authorities' spending. The 1982-1989 consolidation phase – when general government spending, in fact, grew by 3 per cent per year – was characterised by below average expansion of federal outlays, while state and local authority spending grew somewhat faster. Given the Federal Government's political commitments to the eastern Länder, a repetition of such a spending pattern may be difficult, and the target growth of spending may be achieved only if western Länder and local authorities exhibit a higher degree of spending restraint than was the case in the past.

A number of risks attach to such medium-term fiscal projections – all in an upward direction – either leading directly to extra spending or indirectly through increased interest payments: unsettled claims for restitution payments in eastern Germany[29] (although the Government plans to finance these by a property tax in the new Länder), the covering of costs of removing environmental damage, guarantees being called in for Hermes export credits (credits for sales to former CMEA countries)[30], the covering of deficits of the Debt-management fund, additional aid for Eastern Europe and the former USSR, and growing demands on the part of the EC. Moreover, rising capital requirements for Deutsche Telekom are expected, and the railway system could be a large future borrower; and the pension insurance is projected to run very large, though diminishing, deficits in the coming years, unless contributions are increased.

Monetary policy: the quest for financial stability

Faced with the uncertain real economic effects of unification, the unpredictable money demand of eastern German residents and the huge prospective bor-

rowing requirements of the public sector, monetary policy entered uncharted
waters in 1991. Though subject to particular uncertainties, the Bundesbank
adopted a cautious continuation of its policy of monetary targeting by announc-
ing a prolongation of the 4 to 6 per cent target range for the all-German broad
money supply for 1991 with the provision that adjustments of the target could be
required in the light of how the financial integration evolved. As the year went
on, the "normalisation process" of money demand in the new Länder progressed
more rapidly than initially anticipated putting monetary expansion mostly at the
bottom end of or below the target range of 4 to 6 per cent. In response to these
apparent changes in portfolio behaviour in eastern Germany – where part of the
initial "monetary overhang" was shifted into longer-term deposits – the
Bundesbank decided at the mid-year policy review to lower the monetary target
range by 1 percentage point to 3 to 5 per cent.

Diagram 8. **MONEY MARKET DEVELOPMENTS**

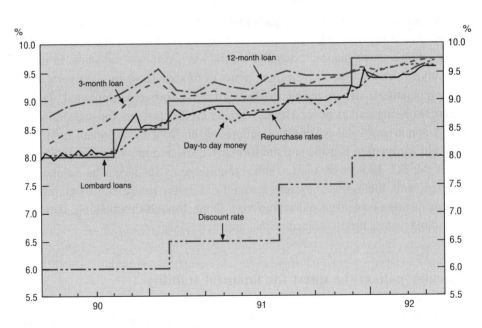

Source: Deutsche Bundesbank, *Monatsberichte.*

44

After having maintained policy-controlled interest rates stable, and allowed short-term money market rates to drift up only moderately from late-1989 to the third quarter of 1990, the Bundesbank subsequently resumed its policy of frequent, small increases in interest rates so as to dampen expansionary pressures in western Germany and to allow for a continuation of the normalisation of east German money demand clawing back some of the initial monetary overhang from conversion[31] (Diagram 8). Thus, following a rise in the discount and Lombard rates in late January 1991, repo-rates were raised in several steps from 8.5 to 8.75 per cent in the first half of 1991, even though the broad money supply grew only slowly.

In the autumn, when monetary growth reaccelerated and short-term interest rates were pushed up to the "Lombard limit", the Lombard rate was raised in August by $1/4$ percentage point and again in December by $1/2$ percentage point to $9^3/4$ per cent, its highest post-war level (if the special Lombard rate applied at times in the early 1970s and 1980s is disregarded). At the same time, the discount rate was increased from $7^1/2$ to 8 per cent. The size of the December interest rate moves surprised market participants and gave rise to some controversy. The economy was apparently softening; the rise in inflation could be said to reflect in large part earlier tax and wage increases, which were not reversible by an *ex post* interest rate hike; and the money supply was within the target range. On the other hand, monetary growth accelerated during the second half of 1991 far above what was felt to be tolerable in the longer run – even if sufficient allowance was made for special factors boosting money growth (see below)[32] it was felt that the monetary authorities should give a clear signal that there would be no accommodation of higher wage inflation and that their anti-inflationary resolve was unchanged.

Earlier in December, the Bundesbank had announced as an intermediate target for monetary policy an increase in the broad money stock of $3^1/2$ to $5^1/2$ per cent between the fourth quarters of 1991 and 1992. This target range was below what had been recommended by the five leading economic research institutes (4 to 6 per cent) whereas its upper limit coincided with the $5^1/2$ per cent proposed by the Council of Economic Experts (Table 16). In deriving the 1992 monetary target, the Bundesbank assumed an increase in the real potential GNP of 2 to $2^1/2$ per cent for western Germany and $3^1/2$ per cent for the eastern German economy. This implied a $2^3/4$ per cent increase in the all-German potential output.

Table 16.   **Monetary targeting for 1992**

Money concept	Bundesbank	Five major Economic Institutes	Council of Economic Experts
	Broad money (M3)	Broad money (M3)	Central bank money
Potential output growth	2³/₄	3	3¹/₂
Normative inflation	2	2	2
Trend in money-income ratio	¹/₂	¹/₂	0
Total	5¹/₄	5¹/₂	5¹/₂
Upper target range	5¹/₂	6	
Lower target range	3¹/₂	4	

Source: Deutsches Institut für Wirtschaft, *Wirtschaftswoche* 7/92.

Maintaining the medium-term price objective with a normative price increase of 2 per cent while allowing for a ¹/₂ per cent trend decline in velocity, and a special deduction for the ample liquidity endowment of the economy at the end of 1991, the mid-point of the range was derived at 4¹/₂ per cent.

Accelerating monetary growth despite higher interest rates

Monetary expansion in 1991 was – as in 1990 – uneven through the year. As noted above, growth of M3 slowed considerably in the early part, influenced by an apparent unwinding of the high liquidity preference exhibited by eastern German portfolio holders in the immediate aftermath of unification. However, as in 1990, money supply growth quickened significantly as the year progressed (Diagram 9). In the last six months of the year, M3 grew at an annual rate of 8 per cent and at an even faster pace (10 per cent) in the last quarter. The concomitant sharp increase in credit demand reflected the emerging recovery of production in eastern Germany, intensified property transactions and a growing squeeze on self-financing capabilities of western German firms. Despite the acceleration of monetary expansion, the adjusted target was overshot only by a small margin.

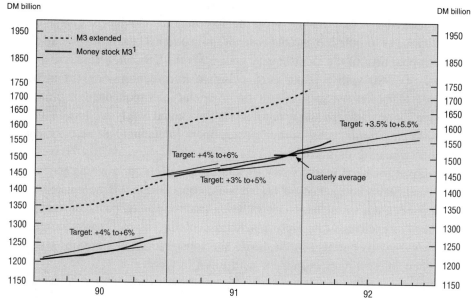

Diaram 9. **MONEY SUPPLY DEVELOPMENTS**
Target and movement to March

DM billion

- - - - - M3 extended
———— Money stock M3[1]

Target: +3.5% to+5.5%

Target: +4% to+6%

Target: +3% to+5%

Quaterly average

Target: +4% to+6%

DM billion

1. Seasonally-adjusted annual rates.
Source: Deutsche Bundesbank, *Monatsberichte.*

In addition to the currency-union effect referred to above, prospective changes in taxation of interest income may have added to the instability of the demand for money. In June 1991, the Constitutional Court ruled that the existing system of taxation of interest income was unconstitutional since it gave rise to widespread tax-evasion, and conceded the government time until the end of 1992 to present an alternative scheme. While there are indications that the court ruling has slowed monetary capital formation for some time and led to currency hoarding and capital exports, it is uncertain how fast and far these effects will be unwound in response to the Government's relatively generous plans for interest income taxation[33]. Finally, demand for Deutschemarks as a parallel currency has boosted the cash component of M3. Thus, the growth of currency in circulation accelerated from an annual rate of 3½ per cent between end December 1990 and end-June 1991 to 13½ per cent between end-June and end-December 1991.

Foreign exchange and capital market developments

Foreign exchange-market developments in 1991 were to a considerable extent shaped by the weakness of the international conjuncture and market expectations as to inflation and the costs of unification. Thus, following an almost uninterrupted drift of the Deutschemark *vis-à-vis* the US dollar from mid-1989 to the end of 1990 with a 6 per cent swing in Euro-deposit rates in favour of DM assets, market reassessment of the budgetary consequences of unification and hope for an early economic recovery in the United States produced a marked decline in the external value of the Deutschemark in the first half of 1991, despite a further widening of the interest rate differential (Diagram 10). However, as international financial markets saw dwindling prospects for a strong recovery in the United States and hence for higher yields on US-dollar denominated assets, the Deutschemark strengthened again. On a trade-weighted basis, movements in the effective exchange rate were much less volatile, as the Deutschemark was stable *vis-à-vis* its partners in the EMU and most European countries tended to move their interest rates in tandem with those in Germany.

Following the rise of bond yields in early 1990, induced by public announcements of the possibility of an imminent German unification, bond yields decreased somewhat until recently, notwithstanding the massive public-sector recourse to the bond market and the progressive worsening of actual inflation (Diagram 11). Investor confidence in the anti-inflationary resolve of the Bundesbank as well as falling yields abroad appear to have made longer-term financial investments increasingly attractive, particularly to foreign investors, and the yield curve became more steeply inverted as the year went on. The policy tightening in December unleashed a rally in the bond market, which brought long-term yields down to 8 per cent, the level in early 1990 prior to the first official announcement of a possible monetary union.

Structural policies: selected issues

Subsidy cutting: difficult first steps

Subsidisation covering direct aid as well as tax allowances declined from about $3^3/_4$ per cent of GNP in the mid-1980s to $3^1/_4$ per cent at the beginning of this decade (Table 17). With unification there was a rise in subsidisation, notably

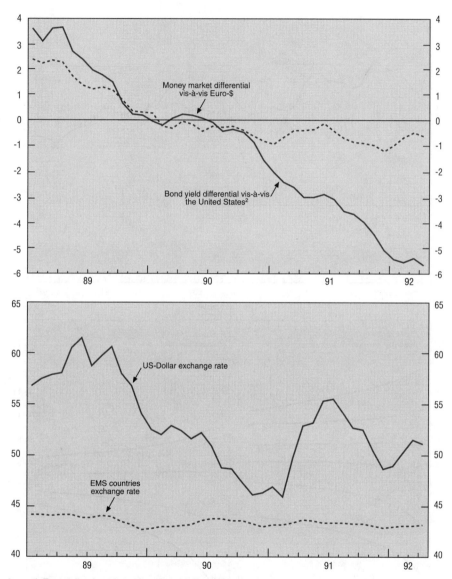

1. 3-month Euro-dollar deposit rate less 3-month Euro-DM deposit rate.
2. Yield on 10-years Treasury bonds in the United States less yield on 10-year Federal Government bonds in Germany.

Source : Deutsche Bundesbank, *Monatsberichte.*

Diagram 11. **THE YIELD STRUCTURE IN THE BOND MARKET**

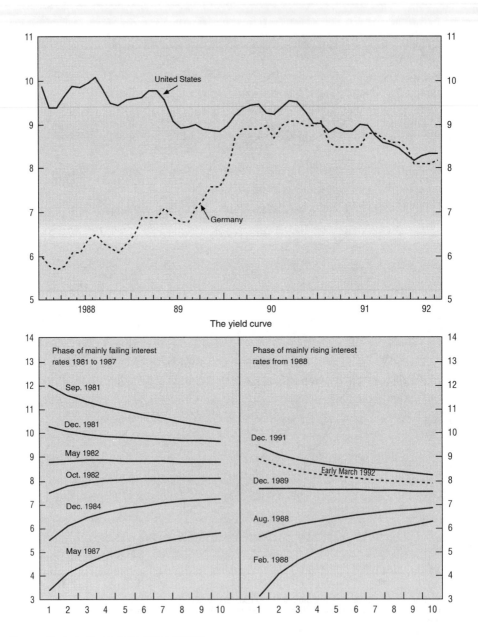

The yield curve

Phase of mainly failing interest rates 1981 to 1987

Phase of mainly rising interest rates from 1988

Source: Deutsche Bundesbank, *Monatsberichte.*

Table 17. **Subsidisation**

DM billion

	1970	1980	1985	1990	1991	1992
Federal government	14.0	24.6	27.6	30.1	38.5	37.7
Financial aid	7.8	12.5	11.9	14.2	21.8	21.7
Tax allowances	6.2	12.1	15.7	15.9	16.6	16.0
Local authorities	13.4	27.3	31.5	34.9	37.6	n.a.
Financial aid	6.8	13.1	13.1	16.2	17.2	n.a.
Tax allowances	6.6	14.2	18.4	18.7	20.4	n.a.
ERP financial aid	1.1	2.7	2.9	5.6	8.0	n.a.
EC market support	2.9	6.2	8.0	9.5	14.9	n.a.
Total	31.4	60.8	70.0	80.1	98.9	n.a.
(As a per cent of GNP)	4.6	4.1	3.8	3.3	3.5	1.2

Source: Ministry of Finance, *Subsidy Report,* October 1991.

at the Federal level (from 1.2 per cent of GNP to 1.4 per cent of GNP), mainly on account of higher direct financial aid to agriculture, goods-producing sectors and housing. For western Germany the total amount of subsidisation was cut in 1991.

Given the persistent pressure for additional spending in the eastern Länder, the need to cut back or to redirect spending from west to east is becoming increasingly felt. Obvious candidates to provide budget relief were support measures for West Berlin and the former internal border regions. Further steps to cut back subsidisation, taken in mid-1991, are intended to reduce subsidisation by DM 10 billion per year for the period 1992 to 1994, relative to an upward sloping base-line.

For agriculture and housing, financial support from the government is set to increase in the coming years: for the former, the possible subsidy-reducing effects of a GATT-round agreement would be offset, at least in part, by national measures, replacing the present price support system by direct budgetary transfers; and in the latter, there are plans to increase tax privileges for owner-occupied dwellings and to expand the social housing programme in the western Länder as well, as housing need has risen considerably in the wake of unification and high immigration. The amount of coal production has been reduced to put a lid on coal subsidies, but the recent take-over of eastern German shipyards by western German firms raises the possibility of renewed pressures for subsidies in this sector.

Privatisation

Privatisation requires both a clear attribution of property rights and the creation of a competitive and regulatory environment that gives new owners and managers appropriate market signals. While this task was made easier in eastern Germany by the full take-over of the western German legislation and the institutional framework, initial difficulties – notably arising from the choice of restitution before compensation and the lack of information concerning the firms under Treuhand control – hampered the early phase of the privatisation process. By the beginning of 1992, 1.2 million applications for restitution of private property had been made, of which only 5 per cent were decided, mainly due to personnel shortages. Furthermore, 150 000 applications for property transfer to municipalities are queuing in the Treuhandanstalt and in the tax administration, with the number expected to rise to 500 000. Moreover, as noted in last year's Survey[34], the pace of privatisation has also been affected by the fact that the Treuhandanstalt is not a passive auctioneer, seeking to privatise enterprises at the earliest opportunity; instead, considerable emphasis has been placed on preserving employment, and on industrial and regional aspects[35].

Nevertheless, after a slow start and internal reorganisation in late 1990, the Treuhandanstalt was able to privatise 6 600 firms by April 1992, ensuring about 1.1 million jobs and planned investments of some DM 130 billion over the next few years. This has involved accepting low selling prices – often even a negative price when grants, debt cancellations, redundancy and other payments are taken into account – in return for firm commitments on jobs and investment targets, specifically written into sales contracts, with penalty clauses. Some evidence suggest that the importance attached to employment guarantee clauses is, *inter alia,* reflected in sales prices[36], as proceeds, close to DM 28 billion, have been much smaller than expected earlier. The present status of Treuhand firms is shown in Diagram 12: of the 11 555 firms, 32 per cent were sold to German companies, 10 per cent were sold via management buy-outs, and 3 per cent to foreign companies (notably to France, Switzerland and Austria). About 6 per cent were returned to their former owners, while 10 per cent of all Treuhand firms have been closed. There are more than 4 700 firms still remaining in the Treu-

Diagram 12. **STATUS OF TREUHANDANSTALT FIRMS**
End March 1992

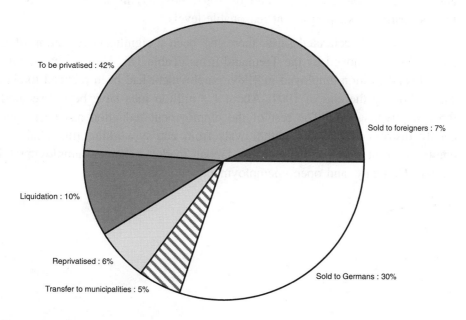

To be privatised : 42%

Sold to foreigners : 7%

Liquidation : 10%

Reprivatised : 6%

Sold to Germans : 30%

Transfer to municipalities : 5%

Note: The total of firms is 11293.
Source: Treuhandanstalt.

Table 18. **Labour shedding in Treuhandanstalt firms 1990-1991**

			In per cent
Employment end 1989	4.1	million	100.0
Employment end 1991	1.65	million	40.2
Reduction	2.4	million	100.0
of which:			
Privatisation (in widest sense)	1	million	41.0
Withdrawal from active working life		220 000	9.0
Change to non-Treuhandanstalt firms		370 000	15.0
Commuters to western			
Germany		270 000	11.0
In labour-market schemes		235 000	10.0
In unemployment		336 000	14.0

Source: Treuhandanstalt.

hand portfolio. In addition, while sectors like retail trade and tourism have been almost fully privatised by the end of 1991, progress in agriculture has been modest, partly to keep prices at reasonable levels.

Parallel to accelerated sales, there has been a significant reduction of the labour force employed by the Treuhand firms (Table 18). Thus, from a total of more than 4 million employed in 1989, employment had been reduced to about 1½ million by the end of 1991. About 1.1 million jobs have been "secured" through privatisations. The rest of the employment reduction has been rather evenly distributed between withdrawals from active working life, change to employment in non-Treuhand firms, labour market schemes, employment in western Germany, and open unemployment.

III. The present situation and projections to 1993

Germany entered 1992 with a level of economic activity below the 1991 average, and, at the time of writing, it is not fully clear that the weakness of demand and output growth in the latter part of 1991 has been entirely overcome, despite a better-than-generally expected outcome for western German output in the first quarter of 1992. In eastern Germany, output of the goods-producing sector stabilised, after a steep fall around the turn of the year and business is becoming less pessimistic in their short term production expectations.

Thus, on a seasonal and calendar adjusted basis, western German real GNP rose at an annual rate of no less than 7¾ per cent from the previous quarter, but this was in part reflecting largely temporary factors: construction activity was (again) benefiting from unusually good weather conditions, and stockbuilding continued to be quite strong, perhaps in anticipation of possible production disruptions associated with unsettled wage negotiations then under way. Growth of private consumption spending was more buoyant than in the preceding quarter, being supported by real disposable income gains and a fall in the savings rate. With imports boosted by the rise in total domestic demand, and a rather moderate rise in exports (including deliveries to the eastern Länder), the change in the net real foreign balance acted as a drag on output growth. While, in a repetition of the pattern from previous years, a technical correction is expected for output in the second quarter, it is uncertain how far that correction will go. However, available short term indicators are not very encouraging: total industrial orders fell in April below the previous year's level and their decline in terms of production months continued. Also, the overall business climate and export expectations deteriorated further, with production cuts being planned for the next three to six months. Even the construction sector has become more uncertain on near term business prospects.

While production indices have moved somewhat erratically in eastern Germany, recent business tendency surveys points to a moderately improving economic situation. In industry, the assessment of near term business prospects has become less pessimistic than in the early months of the year and some increase in production is expected in the coming quarters. The construction sector continues to be the most bullish, with more than half of the firms reporting expectations of rising turnover. There is however a general expectation that labour shedding will continue for some time to come.

Consumer price inflation was quite strong in the spring of 1992. In western Germany, "headline"-inflation has been running at about 4½ per cent (year-on-year) of which ¾ percentage point may be accounted for by the effects of the mid-1991 indirect tax increase. In eastern Germany the cost of living index rose towards the end of the 1991 by some 21 per cent, affected by the withdrawal of subsidies on rent, energy and transports. In the first months of 1992, the index has risen more moderately by about 14 per cent.

Labour market developments, often reacting with a lag to changes in production trends, continued to be quite divergent in the two parts of Germany. After a rise in the first quarter, unemployment in western Germany, seasonally adjusted, edged upwards in the four months to April, being about 100 000 higher than a year earlier. The number of short-time workers rose in the first quarter, but declined in April. With the termination of the special short-time work schemes by the end of 1991, unemployment in eastern Germany rose steeply in the beginning of 1992, but has stabilised recently around 1.2 million, some 15 per cent of the labour force. In April there were around 450 000 short time workers compared with a peak of 2 million in mid-1991.

In western Germany, hourly earnings in the first quarter of the year were increasing rapidly (6½ per cent on a year-to-year basis). With the ending of the eleven-day public-sector strike (the first since 1974), and the settlement concluded for the metal workers, the 1992 wage-round is set to result in economy-wide contractual wage increases averaging 5¾ per cent in 1992 (down from about 7 per cent in 1991).

After having declined in the early months of 1992, the value of all-German exports rebounded strongly in April, while imports over the same period fell somewhat reflecting weakening import prices. For the first four months of 1992, the trade surplus was DM 10 billion compared with DM 6 billion in the same period a year ago. As the service balance registered an important swing of DM 9 billion into a deficit of DM 2 billion, and the transfer balance, though relieved from Gulf war contributions, was in deficit to the tune of DM 18 billion, the resulting current account deficit amounted to DM 11 billion, compared with a deficit of DM 10 billion in the same period in 1991.

Policy assumptions

Fiscal policy: efforts to reduce public sector deficits

Following a better-than-expected outcome for public finances in 1991 – due to stronger tax revenues and underspending in the eastern Länder – the 1992 Federal budget aims at a reduction of the deficit from DM 52 billion (1$\frac{3}{4}$ per cent of GNP) to DM 41 billion (1$\frac{1}{2}$ per cent). Spending growth is to be kept within the 3 per cent ceiling recommended by the Financial Planning Council. However, state and local authority spending is likely to remain vigorous, reflecting high wage settlements in the west and diminishing organisational problems in the regional administrations in eastern Germany, which reportedly have retarded the implementation of spending programmes. While Unity Fund borrowing is planned to decline in 1992 (from DM 31 billion in 1991 to 24 billion), social security finances may show a DM 30 billion swing into a deficit of some DM 11 billion. With tax revenues projected to grow strongly (in the west) the general government deficit may be contained at under 3$\frac{1}{2}$ per cent of GNP in 1992. A considerable part of the reconstruction of eastern German industry and infrastructure is financed off-budget: the Treuhand deficit may swell to DM 30 billion and capital spending of the railways and postal services is also likely to increase significantly. For 1993, the general government financial balance, benefiting from the 1 per cent increase in the general VAT rate and from a strengthening of the eastern German tax base, could stabilise at about the same level as in 1992, hence falling slightly in terms of GNP.

No let-up in the anti-inflationary stance of monetary policy

Faced with accelerating monetary growth and a worsening inflation climate, the discount rate was raised from 7$\frac{1}{2}$ to 8 per cent and the Lombard rate from 9$\frac{1}{4}$ to 9$\frac{3}{4}$ per cent in December 1991. Since then, three-month money market rates

have gradually approached the Lombard-rate level. On the basis of current short-
term interest rates, policy appears tight. However, money and credit growth is
very rapid, and nominal and real long term interest rates are not particularly high.
Monetary expansion has been augmented to an unknown extent by increased use
of Deutschemarks as parallel currency in East European countries, and by portfolio shifts induced by the prospect of the introduction of a withholding tax on
interest increases. Domestic credit demand also grew rapidly reflecting higher
investment activity in eastern Germany and reduced self-financing capabilities of
western German firms.

The 1992 money supply (M3) target growth range (3½ to 5½ per cent) was
based on a normative inflation rate of 2 per cent. Seen in conjunction with the
outcome of the current wage round, and money supply figures showing growth,
even if decelerating a little most recently, well above the upper target limit, this is
very ambitious. However, it underlines the resolve of the monetary authorities to
achieve domestic financial stability over the medium term, and precludes an early
easing of short-term interest rates, even if the economy should remain sluggish
for a time. Following the increase in official lending rates, long-term rates have
fallen to a little over 8 per cent, the level prevailing before the announcement of
the creation of a monetary union between the two parts of Germany.

The outlook to 1993

Given the negative carry-over of growth from 1991 and the deteriorating
business climate until recently, the widely expected resumption of stronger activity in Germany and elsewhere will not make 1992 a year of strong growth.
Overall consumer spending may grow relatively slowly over the projection
period, given the prospect of stagnating employment in the west and of further
job losses in the east (Table 19). Despite rapid growth of labour compensation in
both parts of Germany, high price inflation will importantly limit the advance of
real incomes. A temporary boost to consumption demand in western Germany
will come in the second half of 1992, as the ''solidarity levy'' is withdrawn in
mid-year, and family allowances are significantly improved. However, the higher
general VAT-rate as from 1993 will counteract this stimulus. Despite efforts to
reduce the public-sector deficit, government demand for goods and services will
remain strong: public consumption will continue to grow despite the slimming of

Table 19. **Projections to 1993**

Constant 1991 prices

	Levels in 1991 DM billion			Volume changes, per cent					
	Western Germany	Eastern Germany	Germany total	Western Germany		Eastern Germany		Germany total	
				1992	1993	1992	1993	1992	1993
Private consumption	1 379.1	196.3	1 575.4	1.2	2.4	5.0	3.0	1.6	2.5
Public consumption	469.4	90.2	559.5	1.5	1.2	−4.0	2.0	0.6	1.3
Total investment	578.8	74.8	653.6	1.6	2.8	27.5	13.7	4.5	4.3
Machinery and equipment	569.7	72.4	642.1	0.1	3.4	35.0	18.0	4.2	5.6
Construction	263.8	36.0	299.7	3.0	2.2	20.0	9.0	4.8	3.0
Change in stocks	9.1	2.4	11.5	0.0	0.0	−1.0	2.3	−0.1	0.1
Total domestic demand	2 427.3	361.2	2 788.5	1.3	2.2	6.7	6.6	2.0	2.8
Foreign balance	187.9	−168.1	19.8	0.2	0.4	−5.0	−3.3	−0.2	0.0
Exports	1 009.1	59.2	824.0	3.7	5.1	20.0	15.0	3.5	5.6
Imports	821.1	227.3	804.1	4.1	5.2	9.5	7.0	4.3	5.4
GNP	2 615.2	193.1	2 808.3	1.3	2.3	7.5	9.0	1.8	2.8
Memorandum items:									
Trade									
Intra-German									
Exports	206	38	–	7	7	16	15		
Imports	38	206	–	16	15	7	7		
Balance of intra-trade (DM billion, 1991 prices)	168	−168	–	176	189	−176	−189		
Rest of world									
Exports	803	21	824	3	4	27	31	3.5	5.6
Imports	783	21	804	4	5	3	11	4.3	5.4
Deflators									
Private consumption				4.1	3.5	12.0	8.0	5.3	4.8
GNP				4.5	3.8	19.0	12.0	5.8	4.0
Employment growth	29 173	7 166	36 339	0.0	0.5	−12	−9	−2.5	−1.3
Unemployment ('000)	1 689	913	2 602	1 820	1 840	1 300	1 300	3 120	3 140
Unemployment rate	5.5	11.6	6.7	6.0	6.1	17	17	8.0	8.2

Source: Statistisches Bundesamt, *Volkswirtschaftliche Gesamtrechnungen;* and OECD estimates and projections.

the administrations in the east, and investment spending will be considerable, notably in the eastern Länder. The projected moderate rise in total private investment mainly reflects higher investment in the eastern Länder. A recent Ifo-survey indicates that such investments by western German firms may rise from

DM 14 billion in 1991 to DM 25 billion in 1992. In western Germany, falling capacity utilisation, declining orders and rising pressure on profits can be expected to curb the expansion of business capital formation, notably in 1992. A recent survey covering 400 large industrial companies points to a meagre 1 per cent increase in nominal investment spending for 1992, and a 7 per cent increase in the following year. Stock-building is notoriously difficult to predict, but business tendency surveys suggest that firms are increasingly judging their stocks as being more than adequate. Hence, total domestic demand seems set to grow relatively slowly in 1992, but should pick up thereafter in line with a generally improved world trade picture.

German international cost competitiveness is projected to deteriorate in both 1992 and 1993 (Table 20). However, as the demand pull from eastern Germany diminishes and unused capacity margins widen, western German exporters may intensify their sales efforts in traditional foreign markets, absorbing cost-push pressures in profit margins. Thus with market growth expected to accelerate, German exports should pick up considerably, despite some further market share losses[37]. Growth of eastern German exports will be severely limited in 1992 by the ceiling on export credits to former CMEA countries, but should expand more rapidly in 1993 as trade links with international markets increasingly develop.

With total demand growing more slowly in 1992 and picking-up only little thereafter, the expansion of imports should be more moderate too. This could

Table 20. **International competitiveness, market growth and export performance**

	1990	1991	1992	1993
Manufacturing				
Relative unit labour costs	3.1	−1.7	2.3	1.4
Relative export prices	4.1	−1.2	1.4	1.0
Export market growth	5.3	1.3	6.0	6.8
Export performance	−3.9	−5.2	−1.3	−0.2
Memorandum item:				
Export performance, total goods	−3.7	−4.6	−1.0	−0.3

Source: OECD.

allow all-German real GNP to increase by some 1½ per cent in 1992 and by between 2½ and 3 per cent in 1993. Slow growth of output in *western Germany* (of perhaps 1¼ per cent in 1992) will probably bring to a halt the impressive employment growth recorded in recent years; and with labour supply continuing to grow, unemployment may edge up. In the new Länder, the steepening trend in GNP – output is projected to rise 7½ per cent in 1992 and 10 per cent in 1993 – will raise the level of employment only with a lag as labour shedding may continue into 1993. though at a diminishing pace.

With real net exports increasing over the projection period, and terms-of-trade gains likely, notably in 1992, the trade surplus is set to widen, more than offsetting a higher deficit on the invisible balance. Investment income may shrink significantly in 1992, reflecting lower yields on external assets. Net official transfers, though relieved from the Gulf war contributions, are likely to turn out higher than in 1991 due to increased EC payments and higher aid to Eastern European countries, including the former USSR. The resulting current external deficit should shrink over the projection period, approaching a broadly-balanced position towards the end of 1993.

As noted above, the 1992 wage round seems set to give a 5¾ per cent average increase in western German wages. With the "carry-over" from last year's high settlements this entails a rise of about 6 per cent for the year as a whole. For 1993, the weakening labour market should permit a further reduction of negotiated wage increases. In eastern Germany, wages in many sectors will converge to western German standard wages by 1994-1995, implying continued labour cost increases above productivity advances.

With only a moderate recovery of productivity growth, cost pressures will abate only slowly. However, with overall output growth below that of potential, and continuing low import prices, disinflation is expected to become progressively more manifest. However, recorded inflation will also be markedly influenced by past and prospective changes in indirect taxes: in the second half of 1992, year-on-year changes of consumer prices may decline to between 3 and 3 ½ per cent, due to the disappearance of the "level effect" from the mid-1991 increase in indirect taxes; and in 1993, the 1 percentage point increase in the general VAT rate is estimated to add about ½ percentage point to inflation. In eastern Germany the rate of price increases for tradeable goods should be similar to that in western Germany, while the rise in prices on non-tradeable goods and services will continue to be considerably higher, reflecting not only persistently strong wage cost push but also further upward revisions of administered and subsidised prices. Hence, the rise in the eastern German GNP deflator may well remain in the double-digit range over most of the projection period.

The risks and uncertainties surrounding the current projection concern mainly the outlook for international trade, public finances and inflation. A stronger-than-expected upswing in world trade would impart a welcome positive stimulus to the German economy, but there are concerns that the international recovery could be delayed or provide less of a boost to German exports than built into the present projection. Hence, the net foreign contribution to growth could well be weaker than projected. The rise in the public sector borrowing requirement has been very steep in 1990 and 1991, and the government plans to bring the deficit down to DM 90 billion by 1995. There are, however, possibilities of increased calls on budget outlays: higher EC payments and financial support to Eastern Europe and the CIS countries; payments for past expropriations in the eastern Länder; and higher Treuhandanstalt deficits, which in the final analysis must be included in the government sector. Thus, while contingencies have been made for such events, there is a risk of a rise in public-sector indebtedness beyond current official estimates, which could have adverse implications for financial market confidence, preventing interest rates from falling. Finally, the present projection assumes a ''soft landing'' for inflation, with slowly diminishing costs pressures partially absorbed in profit margins. However, there is a risk that firms will pass more of these cost increases on to prices, making for higher domestic inflation and worsening international competitiveness. In such a scenario, the scope for reduction of interest rates would be more limited and the upturn of economic activity weaker than in the present projection.

IV. The labour market after unification

German economic, monetary and social union in mid-1990 created a labour market with a labour force of some 39 million: over 9 million people in eastern Germany and 30 million in western Germany. As noted in last year's Survey, activity rates in the former GDR were significantly higher than in western Germany. There was a constitutional right to work and employment gave access to certain consumer goods and rights[38]. Unlike in the former Federal Republic, labour hoarding was thus substantial with a chronic excess demand for labour and low productivity.

Since unification, as discussed in more detail in Parts I and II, employment in western Germany has climbed by around one million, following gains of one and a quarter million between mid-1987 and mid-1990, while employment in eastern Germany had fallen below 6½ million (Diagram 13). While the rise in western German employment had practically levelled off by early 1992, as had the fall in unemployment, in eastern Germany the decline appears to have continued unabated into 1992, and open unemployment continues to climb.

As Diagram 13 suggests, the decline in employment would have been much greater without intervention in the labour market; at its peak the special provisions for the short-time working scheme, for example, covered some 20 per cent of the eastern German labour force. As the coverage of this scheme contracted substantially with the termination of the special arrangements at the end of 1991, considerable job losses occurred; these were, however, somewhat smaller than might have been expected, even taking account of the increasing importance of job-creation measures. Part of the fall in employment since unification has been reflected in a shrinking labour force; this is to some extent due to reduced female participation rates but more to older workers leaving the workforce by taking early retirement.

Diagram 13. **THE EASTERN GERMAN LABOUR FORCE**
1989-91

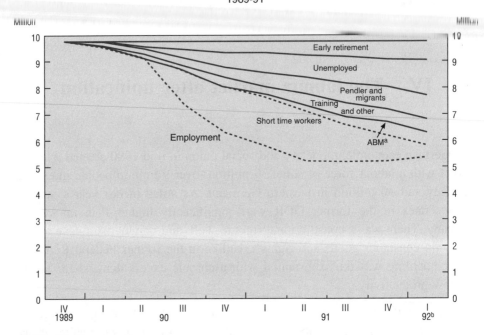

a. ABM = Employment creation measures.
b. estimate.
Source: DIW Wochenbericht 12.13/92 and OECD estimates.

A further important factor preventing the full impact of the decline in employment from falling on unemployment has been labour mobility. By the end of 1991, more than one tenth of the eastern German labour force had either moved to the old Länder to seek work or was commuting to work across the former border. Although many of these *Pendler* (see Part I) commute only relatively short distances – those who live in East Berlin but work in West Berlin are included – many travel considerable distances, one sign that there is much potential flexibility in the eastern German workforce.

Despite such favourable signs, it is clear that substantial labour-market adjustment problems remain in eastern Germany, reflected in the discussion of aggregate output and employment developments in Part I. Mechanisms need to be found to enable labour displaced from non-viable firms to find productive employment elsewhere. The challenge is to minimise the economic costs and social hardship during this process while trying to prevent the development of new rigidities or the strengthening of existing ones. Restructuring and adjustment will be implemented by largely following custom and practices developed in western Germany. In so far as these are embodied in a legal and institutional framework, they were introduced into eastern Germany immediately on unification, supplemented by a number of schemes specific to eastern Germany. In this chapter the structure of labour market institutions and their operation in western Germany are outlined before discussing their functioning in the context of the situation in the eastern German economy and in the light of certain problems that have arisen in the western German labour market.

The development of labour market institutions in western Germany

The principle of collective bargaining between trade unions and employer organisations was first established in Germany in the constitution of the Weimar Republic in 1919. In post-Second-World-War West Germany both social and political consensus maintained the constitutional principle that wages (and most other conditions of employment) are to be determined by collective bargaining between the social partners; government is not to interfere in these negotiations (the principle of "Tarifautonomie"), ruling out the imposition of a legal minimum wage, for example. On the other hand, provisions exist for the enforcement of contracts, even, in certain specific circumstances, among firms not party to the negotiations[39]. The position of labour is reinforced by legal provisions for co-determination ("Mitbestimmung") in enterprises, and by various restrictions of employers' freedom to dismiss employees. While the government plays little active part in relations between private-sector employers and organised labour, its education and training policy has evolved – to some extent in response to problems in the labour market itself – in a manner that can be seen as complementing the other institutions.

Collective bargaining and co-determination

Collective bargaining is generally organised on a regional and sectoral basis between unions and employers' organisations; thus a contract might cover the textile sector in Lower Saxony, or the metalworking sector in North Rhine Westfalia[40]. In practical terms, settlements are often national[41], with many, though not all, basic wage rates common to all regions. These contracts, *Tarifverträge,* set what are essentially minimum basic ("Tarif") wages – differentiated by job grade[42]. *Tarifverträge* cover working time, holiday entitlements, dismissal procedures etc. as well as wages. Their provisions for wages are usually valid for only one year, while other provisions are renegotiated much less frequently. Some 90 per cent of the labour force is covered by one of around 38 000 such contracts. In practice, actual wages paid exceed Tarif wages by a considerable margin. Employers are free to conduct local negotiations with employees provided the minimum conditions are respected. Effective wages are on average 10 to 20 per cent above Tarif wages with a tendency for large companies to pay higher premiums than smaller ones.

The strong institutionalised position of trade unions in the bargaining structure may explain why unionisation levels are relatively low by international standards[43]. A further explanation may lie in the provisions for co-determination, or employee involvement in company affairs. In firms with more than five employees a *Betriebsrat,* or workers' council, can be set up which must be informed and consulted on matters concerning staff policy; the degree of involvement required by law increases with firm size[44]. In addition, all public and many large private companies have an *Aufsichtsrat,* or supervisory board, which appoints the *Vorstand,* or executive board. One third of the *Aufsichtsrat* must consist of employee representatives, or one half in public companies of more than 2 000 employees (in which case at least one third of the employee representatives must be trade union representatives), although the chairman – a shareholder representative – has the deciding vote in the event of ties; there must be at least one director in the *Vorstand* who is responsible for personnel matters and who is usually nominated by the *Betriebsrat.* Employee representation in firms can be organised independently of the unions – though this is not the usual practice – but does not extend to involvement in wage bargaining or industrial action.

Contract enforcement and extension

All firms who are members of organisations party to a *Tarifvertrag* must pay at least this level of wages, and may not discriminate between union members and non-members (a provision applying to all firms). These provisions are enforceable in a system of labour courts distinct from the civil and criminal justice system[45].

Although the principle of *Tarifautonomie* precludes direct government intervention in wage setting, there is a partial exception to this. If either the employers or the unions who were involved in negotiating a *Tarifvertrag* make a request (and provided the contract covers at least half of the workforce in the industry), the Minister of Labour can extend its provisions to the whole industry, covering members and non-members alike of both employers organisations and unions. Such a declaration, or *Allgemeinverbindlicherklärung,* can be made if the minister considers that it would be "in the public interest"[46]. Its operation is generally confined to low-wage or hard-to-organise industries such as the retail and wholesale trade, office-cleaning, textiles and construction. Where unions are strong enough to force employers who are not members of employers' associations to sign contracts which adhere to the terms and conditions agreed, extension laws are irrelevant. On the other hand, extension laws or at least the threat they could be invoked essentially bar from entry new firms which might in their absence be prepared to compete on the basis of lower wages or more flexible working conditions.

Most such declarations concern matters other than wages, such as hours and working conditions[47]; of 507 in force at the beginning of 1992, only 51 concerned basic wages. In certain areas, nevertheless, this provision is to a large extent a substitute for legal minimum wage legislation, since the contract then becomes enforceable in the labour courts (where, for example, an employer organisation could press a case against a non-member company) although, operating by industry, it can be somewhat more flexible than a global minimum. In the retail and wholesale trade sector in 1989, some 500 000 workers in firms not party to the *Tarifvertrag* (out of total sectoral employment of just over 1.6 million) were covered by an *Allgemeinverbindlicherklärung* concerning basic wages[48]. Its impact more generally is hard to assess, and is discussed further below.

Education, training and active labour market measures

The German labour force (both eastern and western) generally benefits from a broader reach of formal education and training than in other major European countries[49]. This is a product of the education and apprenticeship system, and is reinforced at the margin by active labour-market measures, which have grown considerably during the 1980s in response to persistent high levels of unemployment and rising long-term unemployment

While vocational high schools provide full-time vocational education, the apprenticeship system gives the opportunity for young workers to achieve a vocational qualification and at the same time receive some continuing general education[50]. Apprentices generally receive very low pay initially, as much as 50 per cent below the entry-level *Tarif* wage, in return for commitment by employers to permit attendance at outside courses (which are wholly financed by the federal or Länder governments) as well as to give on-the-job training within the firm. The quality of training provided is monitored (this is the responsibility of the Länder governments, who may delegate the task to trade guilds or other organisations) and must reach certain standards for the firm to be permitted to offer apprenticeships.

Active labour-market measures apply to the unemployed or those about to lose their jobs. Training or re-training courses are mainly provided by private sector training companies, chambers of commerce or labour, approved by the Labour Office. Other measures include wage subsidies, which may be offered to companies who employ disabled, older or long-term unemployed people[51]. Job-creation measures also include provision for *Beschäftigungsgesellschaften* ("employment companies"), which can be set up for the specific purpose of providing training and creating jobs for unemployed people by carrying out certain kinds of public works, provided they do not directly compete with the private sector; their wages (paid at the ruling *Tarif* rate, or at the going local rate when there is no *Tarif* applicable) are subsidised by the Labour Office. *Beschäftigungsgesellschaften* have been a very minor part of labour market policy in western Germany, but their role has been much expanded in eastern Germany, where their position has aroused controversy, as discussed below.

The Federal Labour Office[52] has a key role in all labour market policy. In addition to its functions as an intermediary in the provision of training and other measures, unemployment insurance and other benefits are paid through its local agencies, which also act as job-placement agencies. With the exception of artists' agencies, which have always been permitted to make profits, and certain types of executive recruitment ("head-hunting") agencies which have been tolerated for some time and recently legalised following an EC court ruling, the Federal

Table 21. **Expenditure on labour market measures**

	1974	1980	1990	1991	
				Total	East
	Per cent				
Vocational training	9.7	13.5	10.7	10.8	8.3
Wage subsidies	1.2	3.2	3.3	3.5	2.6
Job-creation schemes	3.1	6.0	5.6	7.4	9.2
Integration benefits, ethnic Germans	0.0	2.0	7.6	3.9	0.1
Short-time working allowance	6.4	2.1	2.7	12.6	29.8
Promotion of all year employment	13.3	8.5	2.0	1.8	0.2
Unemployment benefit and aid	35.5	43.9	49.1	37.2	24.1
Maintenance allowance (training)	14.1	6.6	7.0	6.6	4.7
Old-age benefits	–	–	0.8	7.5	17.7
Administration and others	16.6	14.3	11.2	8.6	3.2
	100.0	100.0	100.0	100.0	100.0
Total (million DM)	10 568	22 832	51 946	82 975	33 578
In per cent of GNP	1.1	1.5	2.1	2.9	–

Source: Federal Labour Office, *Arbeitsstatistik,* several issues.

Labour Office has a legal monopoly of job-placement activity[53]. After the EC court ruling, which referred only to executive recruitment, and in anticipation of more general rulings, modification of this monopoly is under discussion[54]. With the above exceptions, the monopoly prevents the existence of intermediaries other than the Labour Office agencies, although this has never restricted the freedom of employers to advertise vacancies or to accept applicants other than those referred by the agencies[55], unlike the practice in some other countries, most notably (until recently) Italy[56].

Strikes, employment protection and social security

It is illegal to strike or to lock workers out while a wage contract is in force. If a contract expires before agreement on a new one, negotiations must continue for at least four weeks (six in the public sector) before a strike is possible. Unions must ballot their members before calling a strike, with a simple majority of votes cast being sufficient.

Some 20 per cent of the western German labour force – principally in the public sector but also such groups as pregnant women and members of workers' councils in private firms – has absolute security of employment. In occupations with such protection the right to strike is either non-existent or severely curtailed. Several laws, however, regulate the dismissal of private sector employees[57] in general. Individual dismissals or those of small numbers (less than five) of people are not generally covered, but when a firm wishes to dismiss larger numbers, it is obliged to install a "social plan." Such a plan, which has to be agreed with the *Betriebsrat,* must take into account the social situation of the persons to be dismissed[58], and specify severance payments. It must prove that the dismissals are in the interest of the continued existence of the company. *Tarifverträge* often specify some or all of the requirements for the social plan, which may include provision for re-training redundant workers or finding them other jobs.

As an experiment in introducing a limited amount of increased flexibility in hiring and firing, the government introduced in 1985 the possibility of employing workers on two-year contracts with no obligation to compensate for dismissal at the end of the two years; re-hiring may not be on a further short-term contract, however. An indication of the potential role of increased flexibility in promoting employment of low-skilled workers is given by the fact that most workers employed under such contracts were low-skilled in sectors with high demand fluctuations. A study[59] estimated that up to 1988 9 per cent of all new contracts were fixed-term contracts and 60 per cent of these were converted into normal, indefinite, contracts. The law, originally to expire in 1990, was extended to 1995. Its form was unchanged, although the Deregulation Commission had recommended relaxing the condition that only one such contract could be offered before permanent employment was offered.

Once a person becomes unemployed, the social security system in the short term is not particularly generous by international standards; measured by the short-term replacement ratio (the ratio of employment insurance benefit to previous net earnings) of about 58 per cent, the German system is ranked tenth among 20 OECD countries[60]. After three years of unemployment, however, (when entitlement to insurance benefits can be expected to have run out in all countries investigated and basic income support is relied upon), the German system pays out (subject to means testing) 85 per cent of what the insurance benefit would have been, and the maximum replacement ratio of just over 50 per cent ranks the highest[61] in the same international comparison[62].

The labour-market situation and adjustment in eastern Germany

With the unification boom now over, and recovery in eastern Germany still far from robust, unemployment in Germany will remain a major issue beyond the immediate future. Unemployment is not a problem that can be handled by labour-market policies alone; the wider macroeconomic setting, including wage determination, and structural policies are at least as important. The dimensions of the problem in eastern Germany are much greater than those faced in the 1980s by the western German economy. This justifies some reconsideration of the appropriateness of the labour market arrangements currently in place.

Although a thorough comparative structural analysis of the economies of eastern Germany and western Germany requires a considerable amount of detailed information[63], the basic imbalance between a large labour surplus and a small viable capital stock in the new Länder is well documented. The capital shortage in eastern Germany is both a question of machinery and equipment in the private and public enterprise sector, and also of public infrastructure and the quality of the housing stock. While labour generally is not in short supply, an important legacy of the former GDR is a definite lack of entrepreneurial and management experience in running firms in a market-oriented economy, as well as some skill shortages in advanced technologies. Notwithstanding these wide divergences between the eastern and western parts of the country (which were initially rather underestimated), expectations have been that catch-up would occur relatively quickly and that it can be brought about with neither major disruption to the western German economy nor any substantial modifications to labour market institutions and practices.

Convergence through the market?

Since the idea is prevalent that the (per capita) income-generating capacity of eastern Germany must converge on that of western Germany, it is worth recalling the market mechanisms which, if left to themselves, would contribute to bringing this about. The initially low level of wages in eastern Germany would remain low, as many non-viable enterprises closed down and unemployment rose. Unemployment and low wages would give rise to two movements: workers would move from eastern to western Germany in search of jobs, at higher wages; while existing enterprises in eastern Germany would be mostly not very profitable, new investment would be highly profitable at low eastern German wages (though profitability might be reduced by infrastructure deficiencies) and hence capital would flow east.

Some changes in wage differentials could be expected: to induce managers to work in the new Länder, their earnings might have to be higher than in western Germany, whereas those of their employees would probably be lower since the majority of easterners would be unwilling or unable to migrate in search of higher wages. As these opposite flows of capital and labour took place, prices would adjust – real wages would rise in eastern Germany and returns to new investment decline, while in the west wage growth would be damped and returns to new investment would tend to rise.

State intervention in this process has arisen from several sources: first is the desire – motivated partly by ideas of fairness and partly by the need to retain support among eastern Germans for the shift to a market economy – to allow the eastern German population to benefit from unification immediately, rather than to receive only deferred returns from all the initial disruption[64]. Second, while theoretically the incentives to invest in the new Länder should be strong, it has been felt necessary to counter the possible effects on investment of uncertainty over the likely success of integration by offering additional financial incentives; such incentives have also been thought necessary to counter the more tangible, though still difficult to measure, effects of the relatively low quality of telecommunications and other infrastructure. In the latter case, although the problem might be more efficiently overcome by using the resources to improve infrastructure directly – indeed considerable resources are already directed to such efforts – there may be limits to the speed with which this can be done[65].

An additional, perhaps more controversial, justification for subsidising investment in eastern Germany has been the desire to avoid the new Länder becoming an area of low-technology, low-wage employment. The stylised description of a pure market mechanism described above would imply that, for some time, investment would occur in eastern Germany to take advantage of relatively low wages. This would tend to perpetuate and possibly extend relatively labour-intensive production methods[66]. However, while in the face of strong pressure for wage convergence the need for closing the gap between real wages and productivity by substantial investment is clear, subsidising investment coupled with high wages does also favour the build-up of an excessively capital-intensive industrial structure. In a region where labour is in surplus – and living standards are being supported by the budget – the main emphasis should be on promoting job-creating and job-preserving investment, and to devote scarce capital resources to education, training and physical infrastructure improvements.

A third motivation for intervention in the market-driven adjustment process is concern about migration. Both investment incentives (to take the capital to the labour rather than move the labour to the capital) and income-support policies in eastern Germany are partly intended to reduce migration flows from east to west. Some worries about such migration may be misplaced. Migration is unlikely to depopulate much of eastern Germany for an indefinite period: while the share of the population accounted for by the new Länder may remain below its initial level, return migration is likely once income and employment opportunities improve. On the other hand, however, there are legitimate fears both of social tension and pressure on space and social infrastructure – housing, education, medical facilities – in western Germany, and of a potential vicious circle in which areas of initially low wages or high unemployment lose their most productive labour, becoming unattractive to inward investment, thereby encouraging further outflows of labour. It may be noted that rapid increases in eastern German wages – with the intention of reducing the differential with western Germany and hence the attraction to migrants – in advance of underlying productivity gains, will not on their own avoid this problem since they are likely to increase unemployment in eastern Germany, which can be a stronger ''push'' than the wage differential ''pull''[67].

The key role played by relative wages in the market-driven process of adjustment highlights the fact that convergence, while being actively and expensively pursued by overall government policy, may be being hindered by labour market developments, in particular by wage determination. If wage levels do not reflect the surplus of labour in eastern Germany, prospective levels of profitability for new investment will be lower, reducing the incentive to invest; the viability of existing plant is also affected, reducing output and employment, with consequent burdens on the social security budget, and diminishing the ability of

73

the eastern German economy to generate domestically some of the funds needed for investment.

Wage determination – collective bargaining and the social partners

It is not, of course, possible to say what the "correct" level of wages in eastern Germany is, from the point of view of employment preservation and job-creation. But the nature of the bargaining which has resulted in the current level of wages and its projected future path has so far had very little relation to the market-driven process described above. This is a product partly of the nature of the bargaining system transferred from western Germany, partly of problems of ownership and control in eastern German enterprises, and partly a result of over-optimistic expectations and misunderstanding of the convergence process.

Western German labour market institutions and practices have developed a certain degree of wage-inflexibility at the micro level, with the ability of workers to "price themselves into jobs" being severely circumscribed[68]. By contrast, those already in employment have a favoured position and are to a considerable extent protected from cyclical fluctuations in economic activity. This creates a lack of incentive on the union side to take into account the unemployment situation[69] and has arguably contributed to the persistence of high levels of unemployment throughout the 1980s.

On the other hand, a perceived advantage of western German wage-bargaining has been its ability to deliver overall settlements which have been relatively sensitive to the general macroeconomic situation, and with generally low levels of strike activity. During the 1980s wage settlements were such that the share of wages in national income declined almost continuously up to 1990 – starting from a relatively high level – and bargaining is conducted against a background of explicit consideration of such aggregates and their consequences for future growth and employment. Such behaviour may also have been responding to the overall level of unemployment (which, despite strong employment growth from the mid-1980s, has remained high because of a similarly strong labour supply growth) but there is little evidence of sensitivity to regional or industrial variation in unemployment, despite the organisation of most collective bargaining along regional lines[70].

Although there is no legal minimum wage in Germany, the legal and negotiating framework around wage contracts tends to establish minimum wages

Diagram 14. **THE GERMAN LABOUR FORCE AND UNEMPLOYMENT
BY LEVEL OF QUALIFICATION**

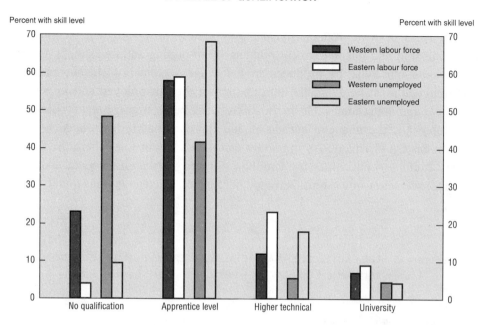

Percent with skill level

Percent with skill level

- Western labour force
- Eastern labour force
- Western unemployed
- Eastern unemployed

No qualification   Apprentice level   Higher technical   University

Sources: Materialien aus der Arbeitsmarkt- und Berufsforschung no. 7/1990(p23) IAB Kurzbericht 12.12.1991.

by industry; settlements have often tended to increase basic wages for the low skilled more than for the higher paid, tending to compress the wage structure[71]. A natural consequence of this would be relatively higher unemployment among those, normally unskilled, people who would otherwise take low-paid jobs. The unskilled are indeed over-represented in the pool of western German unemployed, accounting for almost one half of job-seekers but less than a quarter of the labour force (Diagram 14); in eastern Germany, very few have no formal skills and the burden of unemployment has fallen disproportionately on those with apprentice level qualifications. The response has been increased efforts to train and re-train workers to help bring their productivity in line with wages.

Convergence and catch-up settlements

This response willy-nilly takes high and rising wages as given, letting them reveal areas of low productivity and unprofitable jobs and then tackling the resulting skill and unemployment problem by retraining and investment. Output that would otherwise be produced in low wage sectors is lost, and adequate public funds must be available both to support the unemployed and to provide effective training schemes. Given the discrepancy between wage and productivity developments, the financial burden of this approach has turned out to be very high in eastern Germany. An important part of the labour force there (by far the largest example – encompassing 1 million workers – is that of the metal-workers, often a pace-setter in western Germany because of its coverage of around 4 mil-

Diagram 15. **THE EASTERN GERMAN METAL WORKERS' CATCH-UP SETTLEMENT**

Entitlements in eastern Germany as a percentage of those in western Germany

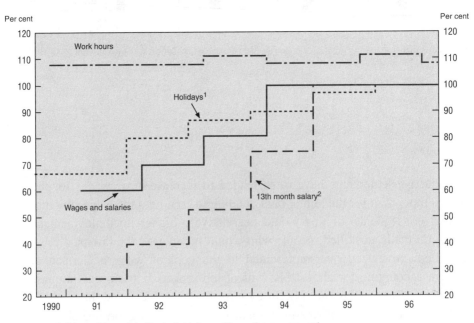

1. Minimum holiday entitlement (estimated); higher entitlements are preserved.
2. 13th month salary and holiday payment (estimated).
Source: Submission from the Ministry of Labour.

76

lion employees) is covered by wage contracts which specify a timetable for convergence with western German *Tarif* wage levels by the end of 1994 (Diagram 15).

The importance of negotiated levels for *Tarif* wages should not be exaggerated. In western Germany there has always been a large difference between basic wages and wages actually paid. As noted above, this gap is typically 20 per cent or more, but is not uniform across sectors[72] (Diagram 16). Though effective wages are somewhat more flexible than *Tarif* wages[73], this is not a great source of flexibility within western Germany in the short term, however, because it is rare for increases in basic rates not to be matched by changes in effective earnings. But with the gap between basic and effective wages not generally so large in eastern Germany, this is a factor which will still allow quite substantial differences in wage levels between the two regions of Germany, even after full convergence of *Tarif* wages. Hours of work, holiday entitlements and holiday pay (including the payment of a thirteenth or even a fourteenth month of salary) may also vary. A further danger of attaching too great an importance to *Tarif* wage levels is that there are in fact a great many *Tarif* wages – as many as there are job grades defined in different industries. Employers have some discretion over the grade into which new employees are taken: many of the migrants or *Pendler* working in western Germany are working at lower grades than correspond to their formal qualifications.

Despite these caveats, the catch-up settlements will tend to generate a path for earnings most unlikely to be justified by productivity growth except with continuing substantial job losses even after the initial shake-out. The negotiations leading to such settlements were conducted, as usual, between the social partners, and the agreements were reached without major conflict. But because the pre-existing eastern German unions were tainted by association with the former regime, the workers were *de facto* represented for the most part by western German unions in the early stages of the process of setting up branches in the new Länder. Under such circumstances the criticism that unions are more interested in the employed than in the unemployed is reinforced by the likelihood that they also took account of repercussions on the employment and earning prospects of western German workers. Since the new Länder are potentially a source of severe wage-competition, workers in western Germany have a clear interest in seeing a fast wage-catching-up process in that region.

Diagram 16. **TARIF AND EFFECTIVE WAGES IN WESTERN AND EASTERN GERMANY, BY INDUSTRY**

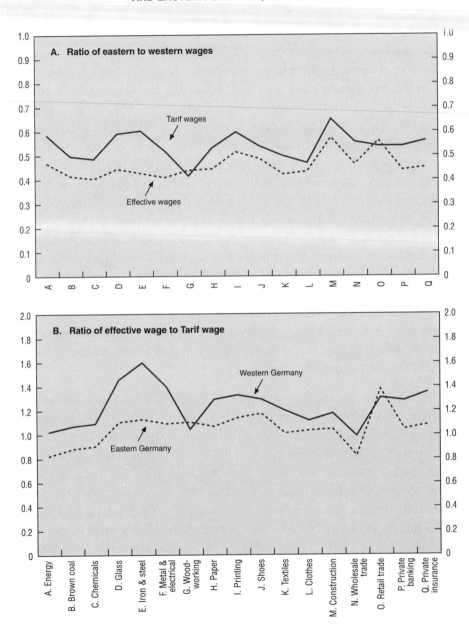

Sources: Federal Ministry of Labour and Social Policy and OECD estimates.

Likewise, employers were also represented by newly introduced western German employers' organisations, who, for very similar reasons, would not be keen to see large numbers of low-cost competitors emerge on their doorstep. Local employers in the east, who might have been expected to resist such reasoning, were only weakly represented; managers themselves were often on short-term contracts and many lacked personal incentives to keep wage costs down[74]. The Treuhandanstalt, as ultimate owners of most industrial firms at the time, did not appear to intervene in managers' decisions, despite the implications of high wage settlements for firms' profitability and potential for privatisation.

This policy was no doubt motivated by the Treuhand's desire to operate a "hands-off" approach to its relations with the management of its firms, and possible fear of being castigated for violating *Tarifautonomie* if it interfered with wage bargaining (not to mention the fact that Treuhand management resources and information systems were themselves overstretched). On the other hand, and in particular in view of the fact that most employment in Treuhand firms has been subsidised up to now in various ways, and because of the management deficiencies and conflicts of interest just discussed, it would have perhaps been appropriate to make more effort to keep wage costs down.

It is not suggested that western German representatives in both sides of industry deliberately acted against the economic interest of the new Länder. The problem has been rather that the wage-bargaining institutions, by placing rather little weight on the economic situations of individual firms[75], effectively ignored the fact that most eastern German firms were barely viable at current wage rates. Large increases in wages in the first year after unification are understandable, even if detrimental to the short-term prospects of the regional economy; in the transition to a market economy from a system where prices meant rather little it is not surprising if prices (including the price of labour) are subject to wide swings in the early stages. But the settlements which provide for complete catch-up with western levels (even allowing for the gap between basic and effective wages) are problematic, because they pre-empt any re-adjustment of wages in the light of economic events.

These settlements are based on the expectation that the economies of the two regions will converge relatively quickly, but they are not conditional on that convergence[76]. Worse, by running ahead of underlying productivity potential[77], such wage increases are likely to slow the very process which would otherwise validate them. Investment is likely to be discouraged, perhaps in favour of investment in other low wage countries in the EC or in eastern Europe. The best that is likely to be achieved is reasonable average productivity growth, but low output growth, with the consequence that mass unemployment, particularly long-term unemployment among older workers and among those unable to acquire sufficient skills, would last even longer.

However, less than 1½ million eastern German workers (less than a quarter of the total workforce, but a much higher proportion of workers in the industrial sector) are so far covered by full catch-up settlements[78]. Furthermore, in certain areas, workers in firms faced with the possibility of liquidation are willing to consider the idea of taking wage cuts in return for some stake in the future of the firm. With the current legal arrangements, such schemes could be at risk if such firms are members of employers' organisations that have signed catch-up settlements, or if unions or employers organisations sought a declaration of *Allgemeinverbindlichkeit*. Avoiding the further spread of catch-up settlements and enabling local initiatives to safeguard the viability of individual firms would be a useful step towards promoting the market-driven catch-up process itself.

Since the main problem with catch-up agreements is their inflexibility – convergence justified by output and productivity growth is to be welcomed – alternative ways to give workers a share in the benefits of adjustment without jeopardising the adjustment process itself need to be sought. This implies some method of linking employee reward to company performance, which could be done by formal or informal profit-sharing or by giving a direct stake in the firm or simply by enterprise-level bargaining. Already in western Germany the latter method is used in some agreements, where part of wage or salary payments are made in equity-type form[79]. This form of employee involvement may be more attractive in the transition from communism than more direct profit-sharing arrangements, although the latter could be more easily spent for immediate improvements in the standard of living.

Social security and employment-creation measures

Unemployment benefit

The social "safety net" also plays an important role in labour market functioning, and the design of training and work-creation schemes can have effects on private sector investment and wage developments. As described earlier, the western German ratio of unemployment benefit to wages is not particularly high by international standards – except when calculated for longer periods of joblessness, so that it may be a relevant factor in analysing long-term unemployment. However, a modification to the scheme applied in eastern Germany may add to the upward pressure on wages. While in western Germany both unemployment insurance benefits and the subsequent means-tested benefits are calculated as a percentage of last earnings (linked to increases in pensions, which themselves are periodically adjusted to take account of inflation and rising real wages) in eastern Germany the benefit yardstick, pensions, are revised upwards almost as fast as actual wages (currently every six months).

This is a reasonable attempt to ensure that those who lost their jobs in the early stages of transition, who were to some extent arbitrarily chosen, are not treated unfairly compared with those made unemployed somewhat later or those remaining in employment. But if wage increases run substantially ahead of productivity, the system is likely to mean both that the budgetary costs of financing unemployment benefits will rise faster than eastern German output and hence increase the need for public sector transfers from west to east, and that the incentive to take a job at a wage rate that a competitive firm can afford will diminish. As far as overall budgetary costs are concerned, they form part of the process by which transfers from western Germany protect living standards in the new Länder and allow them to some extent to borrow against future rises in production. It is perhaps too early to say that these costs to the public sector have become excessive, but a policy with such potentially large costs to both public finance and structural developments needs to be carefully assessed.

Employment maintenance schemes

As the potential for very high levels of unemployment in eastern Germany became clear, employment protection, job creation and training measures in the new Länder have assumed particular importance. Although policy-makers have explicitly rejected general employment subsidies as an appropriate response to a situation of surplus labour and tended to subsidise capital instead, various *de facto* selective schemes to support employment were used in the first eighteen months after unification and, on a reduced scale, are still in operation.

The most important of these were the special generous short-time working arrangements, which allowed, in extreme (but common) cases, a large part of wages to be paid by the state for workers who were producing nothing. At its peak, this scheme covered nearly 2 million workers and was withdrawn at the end of 1991, six months later than originally intended. In addition, the system of guarantees for credits on exports to eastern Europe and the former Soviet Union acts *inter alia* to support employment. The financial cost is uncertain, depending on whether the indemnities that eventually have to be paid by the government exceed the fees paid by exporters. The Treuhandanstalt also provides financial support to employment, though in ways that are very difficult to quantify: its terms of reference oblige it to take into account the social consequences of any employment losses. There is some evidence that this has led both to discounting privatisation sales prices to increase the number of jobs guaranteed and to an extreme reluctance to close non-privatised firms, with continuing operating losses being covered by "liquidity credits" guaranteed by the Treuhandanstalt and with the likely consequence of higher restructuring costs in the future. Both of these hidden subsidies increase the borrowing requirements of the Treuhandanstalt (see above, Part II)[80].

In addition to protecting employment, measures to reduce the labour force through early retirement have reduced open unemployment quite considerably. While the normal statutory retirement ages in Germany are 65 for men and 60 for women, special provisions for eastern Germany introduced in October 1990 allowed people becoming unemployed to enter "pre-retirement" at age 57. Under these provisions, availability-for-work tests were no longer applied to establish entitlement to unemployment benefits. In July 1991 eligibility was widened to include those aged 55 and over, and the scheme extended up to July 1992. Almost 400 000 people withdrew from the labour force under these provisions by the end of 1991 in addition to some 330 000 who had applied for early retirement between February and October 1990[81].

Employment creation and training

With the withdrawal of many of the initial activity and income-supporting schemes, the role of employment creation and training has become more prominent. The system developed in western Germany, where active labour market measures were particularly expanded during the 1980s, was introduced along identical lines in eastern Germany. For much of 1991 most such new training amounted to little more than unemployment benefit by another name, as the quality of training was rather low. This has been attributed to the haste with which training companies were set up and the difficulty of vetting their competence – the network of local labour office agencies, responsible for such vetting, was being set up more or less at the same time.

While the situation as regards the quality of training should gradually improve, the size of the task, and pressure to keep the headline unemployment total low will inevitably lead to some strains. In one area – the *Beschäftigungs-gesellschaften* – there is already some controversy. These "employment companies" exist mainly to provide practical training for their employees[82], and have typically been set up from non-viable parts of Treuhandanstalt firms. They currently absorb some 13 per cent of funds available under employment-creation schemes.

Most *Beschäftigungsgesellschaften* are small – on average five to six employees per firm. Administrative costs in such cases are quite high. A number (some 400 by the spring of 1992) of larger firms have been set up to try to keep average costs down, though at the obvious risk of being more likely to upset the balance between private and public enterprise in local markets. Nevertheless, costs in *Beschäftigungsgesellschaften* in eastern Germany seem high. While average comparable wages in eastern Germany were estimated at some 60 per cent of the western Germany level in late 1991, the average cost of the wage subsidy per worker in employment companies in eastern Germany was over 70 per cent of that in western Germany[83]. Initially, not only wage costs were directly paid for by the Labour Office (as in western Germany) but also non-wage operating and certain equipment costs. As such costs were seen to increase to more than half of total costs during 1991 (the Upswing East programme, federal and Länder governments also pay certain costs), subsidy availability was restricted and from 1992 onwards, direct subsidies were replaced by subsidised loans to cover such costs.

The employment companies perform a variety of tasks related to improving, cleaning up or renovating industrial buildings or sites, projects which are directly funded by the Federal Labour Office. Controversy has arisen over the extent to which these companies compete unfairly with private sector companies which might also be capable of carrying out this work. This problem applies more generally to employment creation measures, where the Labour Office provides support in the form of paying directly the wages of some or all workers on certain projects.

The criticism of these arrangements, which in a sense amount to a selective employment subsidy, is that they may stifle the development of private enterprise, particularly as they pay the same wages as a private company would have to pay[84]. The *Beschäftigungsgesellschaften* themselves may have little incentive to improve their own efficiency, since they do not have to compete with the private sector, as the finance comes through the Labour Office which, by its constitution, cannot provide money other than as a subsidy for employment on projects which it must approve individually.

An alternative to tying financial support to one group of suppliers would be for project finance to be made available to, for example, local communities. This would enable them to choose the work to be carried out and to allocate it by competitive tendering, thereby stimulating competition and the development of private enterprise. Up to now, apart from legal restriction on the use of unemployment insurance contributions, lack of administrative resources in local government, compared with a now well-developed network of agencies of the federal Labour Office has been a major obstacle to this approach. But since *Beschäftigungsgesellschaften* will probably be an important element in labour market policy in eastern Germany for some time, such considerations of dynamic efficiency become at least as important as the short-run benefits of reducing unemployment. From the worker's point of view, too, the employment companies may hinder initiative, since there is unlikely to be any monetary incentive to look for employment in the private sector, which may be less secure[85].

The Labour Office has been sensitive to criticism that these measures stifle private enterprise, while claiming that clear examples of such effects are very few – funds for employment-creation schemes are intended to cover only activities which would not otherwise take place. In the autumn of 1991 a scheme was introduced whereby the relevant local chamber of commerce is consulted over all projects and can veto them if capable local enterprise would be crowded out. The employers' organisations have suggested that policy should go further in organising competitive tendering where possible. They also advocate that employment companies (and other employment creation schemes) should pay wages below the contractual Tarif wage but above unemployment benefit, preserving some incentive for workers to move to the private sector, as well as an incentive not to remain unemployed. While the extraordinary circumstances of the difficulties in eastern Germany justify extraordinary measures in response, questions of cost minimisation and efficiency cannot be ignored. Such suggestions would be a useful way of working to improve the efficiency, and to reduce the cost, of what is becoming a key part of this response.

Overview

Since unification, labour-market policies and institutions have been subject to conflicting pressures. On the one hand, they provide the means by which much of the income and employment support for the new Länder is delivered. Given the magnitude of this support, it is clear that some distortion to market incentives was unavoidable, but there are areas of current policy where such distortions could be reduced. On the other hand, labour-market policy must contribute to promoting and assisting the adjustment of the labour force to this very set of unfamiliar incentives. Part of this adjustment should be brought about by wage bargaining that is responsive to differences in supply and demand conditions between the eastern and western Länder and in individual markets. In principle, the regional and sectoral structure of bargaining common in Germany should be able to provide a good deal of this flexibility, but practice in western Germany has tended to produce little such differentiation in settlements, and in 1991 the first eastern German wage round headed clearly in the wrong direction, paying more attention to divergences in living standards than to divergences in productivity. Wage bargaining practices, labour market laws and regulations have developed in western Germany so as to provide considerable protection to employees against excessive cyclical and lifetime fluctuations in wages and employment. By promoting social peace and coherence this institutional setting has probably contributed to creating an environment conducive to stability and growth. However, confronted with the need for major structural adjustments, of a degree not seen in western Germany since the late 1940s, its contribution to a smooth integration of the two economies has been less successful.

V.   Conclusions

The huge gap in productivity levels between the two parts of Germany, which had opened up cumulatively during the more than 40 years of post-war division, widened further during the first year after unification. While the western German economy expanded rapidly under the impact of positive demand and supply-side impulses, the abrupt and full exposure of the run-down eastern German economy to competition from both western Germany and from abroad together with strong pressure for wage convergence and the breakdown of traditional export markets destroyed the viability of large parts of industrial capacity. Despite large-scale financial support measures, there was a sharp contraction of output and employment. A turning point was, however, reached a year ago for both economies: in the east the steep fall of production bottomed out around mid-year, when the post-unification boom in the west had just passed its peak. Since then there has been a partial recovery of activity in eastern Germany, notably in construction-related activities and small businesses, while the contraction of employment has continued; in western Germany, starting from very high levels of capacity use, output registered a decline during the second half of last year but appears to have been regaining the lost ground in the early months of this year.

Looking ahead at the remainder of 1992 and further into next year and allowing for policies already taken or announced, the prospects are for a recovery of economic activity from the recent pause in western Germany, with growth picking up to more than 2 per cent during the year: the solidarity surcharge on income tax is to be lifted in mid-year, and fiscal and monetary policies are set to support a more sustainable rate of growth than during the recent boom. Continuing recovery in the new Länder may take all-German growth to between 2½ and 3 per cent in 1993. Although accelerating world trade in 1993 will mean a stronger contribution from exports, domestic demand will remain restrained: the 1 percentage point VAT increase in January 1993 will affect real consumption while high interest rates, lower profits and below-potential growth will dampen investment (already at high levels) in western Germany. In eastern Germany, demand growth will continue to be largely supported by public sector transfers and increasing investment expenditure. With output in western Germany growing below potential and labour shedding in the east continuing, though at a reduced rate, unemployment is likely to rise.

Following the expiry of moderate three-year wage contracts in 1990, subsequent wage settlements in western Germany have led to a steepening of "home-made" inflation despite some easing of pressure on resources since mid-1991. Wage agreements for 1992 show some moderation but, given the projected low growth of productivity, there will be little relief on the cost side. However, with output growth projected somewhat below that of potential and continuing low growth of import prices, disinflationary tendencies should gradually become more manifest, bringing the annualised rise in the private consumption deflator – net of the effects of the VAT increase in 1993 – perhaps down to $2\frac{3}{4}$ per cent or less by the end of next year. For eastern Germany, the intention to catch up with western German wage levels has set most wages on a track until the mid-1990s far beyond that warranted by likely productivity developments. Hence the rise in the GNP deflator there may well remain in the double-digit range over most of the projection period.

The sharp contraction of output and gainful employment in eastern Germany has led to measures to protect employment, induce investment and provide income to those having lost their jobs. As a result, the overall public finance position has deteriorated: despite tax increases, the general government deficit on a national-accounts basis was two-thirds higher in 1991 than in 1990, attaining DM 77 billion or $2\frac{3}{4}$ per cent of GNP, and is set to rise further in 1992.

The extraordinary circumstances of the post-unification adjustment process justify extraordinary measures, at least for a time. Thus, running a substantial budget deficit near the peak of the (western German) business cycle is not in itself a sign of overspending or weakness of the tax system nor a situation that should not be corrected eventually as the process of catch-up in eastern Germany progresses. But this does not mean that the messages given by the mounting debt and costs of debt servicing can be ignored: the rules of arithmetic with respect to the dynamics of debt-GNP ratios and the relative burden of interest payments still apply. Moreover, it is arguable that the current level of transfers of resources per head of the eastern German population, equivalent to about one quarter of western German per capita GNP, is as high as, if not higher than, can reasonably be expected to be raised without generating negative incentive effects on either the providing or receiving end. Expenditure on income support that does not produce real investment in human or physical capital will tend to weaken economic incentives and discourage initiatives in the new Länder. Support programmes should be assessed in this light, working wherever possible to promote the development of an entrepreneurial culture.

Given recent trends in general government borrowing and continued financing requirements of the Treuhandanstalt, it is clear that determined measures are required to keep the underlying fiscal position under control. It is encouraging to note that overall budget deficits turned out to be smaller in 1991 than expected at the beginning of the year and that the Government seems firm in its intention to implement its tough medium-term budget consolidation programme. Official targets are to bring the deficit of the federal government down to DM 25 billion by 1995 and that of the territorial authorities to DM 80 billion by restraining nominal federal spending to 2 1/2 per cent per annum and that of the western Länder and local governments to 3 per cent. This would mean that total public-sector debt – including liabilities of the Treuhandanstalt and the public housing sector in the new Länder but excluding public enterprises – could reach 50 per cent of GDP by the mid-1990s, compared with less than 38 per cent for the former Federal Republic in 1982, just before the previous period of consolidation. Interest payments alone may then absorb 1 to 1 1/2 per cent of GDP more than in 1989. Meeting these targets will call for considerable consolidation effort at all levels of government, requiring a shift in the primary budget balance in terms of GDP of 2 per cent to be achieved in just three years; this compares with an improvement of 4 per cent recorded in the eight years to 1989. It is important to achieve this shift, which should then allow a gradual decline in the ratio of debt to GDP in the latter half of the decade.

The catching-up process in eastern Germany should eventually generate considerable tax revenues, which will contribute to servicing the debt currently accumulating as a result of policies to support living standards and encourage economic development there. However, this will be insufficient on its own to meet the 1995 target. The pressure to reduce subsidies in western Germany must be maintained, though even ''breakthroughs'' in this area may in practice take time to make major contributions, underlining the importance of the recent decision to extend the moratorium on debt-financed new spending or tax relief programmes beyond the current year. It is also important to arrest the recent tendencies of state and local government spending in the western Länder to rise faster than federal spending and of social security outlays to exceed current revenues. The revised finance equalisation system, due in 1995, may be an opportunity to ensure that the former tendency does not undermine budget consolidation efforts at the general government level.

Monetary policy should remain focused on the objective of restoring price stability – taken to be annual price increases in the range of 0 to 2 per cent. By maintaining a "low" target for monetary growth for 1992, the authorities have signalled their unwillingness to provide monetary accommodation of what are considered excessive increases in wage costs or a pass-through of such costs on domestic prices. However, the currently rapid money and credit growth has given rise to concern that, if it continues, it may impair the credibility of the monetary authorities by allowing inflationary pressure and expectations to remain strong. However, some of the recent excessive growth of money and credit may be due to cyclical and other special factors, as discussed in Part II. First, the possibility that unification has fundamentally changed at least the short-run behaviour of monetary aggregates more than allowed for cannot easily be dismissed. Second, higher credit demand could have arisen from the reconstruction of eastern Germany. Third, prospects of the introduction of a withholding tax on interest income may have affected portfolio behaviour. Finally, there is evidence of increased Deutschemark hoarding and the use of the Deutschemark as a parallel currency in the East European countries. Against this background, a temporary above-target monetary expansion would not seem to call for further tightening of monetary conditions, but there should be no let-up in the pursuit of lower inflation, even if this means high interest rates for a prolonged period: only a firmly based decline in the underlying rate of price increases would create the scope for lowering policy-controlled lending rates.

Reflecting high investment demand arising from unification rather than low domestic savings, the current external balance in 1991 registered a deficit of some 1½ per cent of GNP, a swing of 4½ per cent since 1990. While unusual for Germany, running current external deficits for some time should not give rise to concern. The diversion of exports and the massive sucking-in of imports are consequences to be expected from sustaining living standards in the new Länder during the reconstruction period and from high rates of capital formation. The high rate of domestic resource use has helped to sustain world trade and hence economic activity in partner countries, though there have been dampening effects from the high degree of interest rate dependence on Germany among many European countries. And in Germany, increased competition from imports will help to stabilise prices.

The swing in the balance of payments, the mounting budget deficit and difficulties in monetary management are all direct or indirect manifestations of the problems that have arisen from integrating the new Länder into the western German economy. The restoration and maintenance of sound overall economic balance depend to a large extent on generating a self-sustaining recovery in eastern Germany. A major preoccupation since unification has thus been to develop a market-based private enterprise economy in eastern Germany, a process that has been centred around the Treuhandanstalt. The high rate of privatisations and the smoothness with which this has been achieved is a major policy success and a vindication of what seemed over-optimistic expressions of intent in early 1991. However, revenue raised by privatisation has been far below what had been hoped for in the autumn of 1990. The need to sell quickly and the desire to obtain employment and investment commitments led to low net sales proceeds, taking account of liabilities for environmental costs, social plans and debt write-offs. In the event, the financial deficit of the Treuhandanstalt has been running at around 1 per cent of GNP.

The Treuhandanstalt was designed to have a limited life – its borrowing authorisation covers the period to the end of 1994. Continued efforts to wind up its business quickly remains important with more emphasis than in the past given to budgetary control and promotion of management skills which are in short supply at the moment. One way to work towards these goals is to make more frequent use of partial privatisation, in which the Treuhandanstalt retains a passive minority equity stake in firms where managers without sufficient resources take a part stake, or are perhaps employed on profit-sharing management contracts. By sharing some of the risk – and therefore reducing the need for a risk-discount on the selling price – the Treuhandanstalt might reduce its net debt in the medium term and thus ease the budget consolidation process. At the same time, it must ensure that the "hard budget constraint" is effective in non-privatised companies, which should not be supported if they have no clear prospect of viability. Risk-sharing arrangements may lead to a longer life for the Treuhandanstalt as a state holding company, with the potential danger of encouraging a "soft budget constraint" mentality. Effective arm's length relationships and controls would need to be established to enforce a hard budget constraint and to avoid the Treuhandanstalt injecting fresh capital rather than selling off its holdings over time. Whatever the mode of privatisation, it remains important to find quick ways to remove property rights uncertainties, or at least their retarding effects on privatisation and restructuring, which reportedly affect some three-quarters of the remaining Treuhand-owned enterprises.

To what extent labour-market institutions have influenced structural adjustment in western Germany is not easy to say. This Survey has considered their appropriateness during the current transition process in eastern Germany where the answer seems clearer: judged by the outcome for wages, which have risen far above levels justified by current productivity potential, wage bargaining in 1990-1991 was too remote from the realities of the balance between supply and demand for labour in the new Länder. The newness of the negotiating unions and employers' organisations to eastern Germany, and the fact that there were conflicting objectives and interests on both sides, contributed to this. But inherent in the system is a low degree of responsiveness to the market position of individual firms, branches of industry or regions, and this has had a negative impact on aggregate wage developments, encouraging the persistence of unrealistic expectations.

Given the potential for rapid productivity increases from even small investments in improved organisation and management, one year of excessive wage growth could be relatively easily offset if wages stopped running ahead of labour efficiency gains. However, the major obstacles here are the existing catch-up settlements and expectations for wage increases which are based on incomplete understanding of how economic convergence is to be achieved. Overall wage catch-up is dependent on substantial new investment which will occur rapidly only if wages provide an attractive cost environment initially: this attracts external investment directly while also encouraging greater production with existing capital, ensuring higher levels of employment and allowing investment to be financed by the build-up of internal savings. These economic relationships are well understood by many already. Indeed, a recent joint report of the five major

91

economic research institutes called for eastern German employers to take advantage of existing revision clauses and to renegotiate last year's catch-up settlements. Such a development would run counter to tradition but, as noted above, extraordinary circumstances justify extraordinary measures.

Just as Treuhand policy, after the initial urgency of privatisation, needs to be tempered with budgetary and efficiency considerations, so too do employment preservation and creation measures. The running down of the short-time working scheme has reduced financial support to employment and labour hoarding. Employment-creation measures have expanded rapidly to fill the gap. Since a significant part of the labour force will be involved in employment-promotion schemes this year, either full or part time, the private-sector labour market, as well as the enterprise sector, is bound to be affected. It is thus important to ensure that these measures, and in particular employment companies (*Beschäftigungsgesellschaften*), which are established on private initiative but draw considerable financial support from the Federal Labour Office, are organised so as to obtain the maximum benefit in terms of training and adaptation of the labour force to the market economy, and that they do not impede the development of private firms offering services at prices reflecting the full costs of providing them. However, the direction of employment support through such measures should itself be of limited duration. It would also be desirable that the institutions which can benefit from services provided through employment-creation schemes be financially enabled to put projects out to tender, perhaps with some permitted bias in favour of local suppliers.

Given the large contribution of employment-creating measures to total employment in eastern Germany, consideration should also be given to the level of wages received by workers on such schemes. Normally the relevant *Tarif* wage is paid, which in western Germany would usually be well below the market wage. In eastern Germany, however, the gap between *Tarif* and effective wages is small, and *Tarif* wages themselves are frequently higher than justified by potential productivity. This means that there is a much greater danger of employment creation measures putting a floor on wages and discouraging people from taking lower-paying jobs in the private sector. To avoid this, consideration should be given to paying those covered by employment-creation measures rather less than *Tarif* wages.

To sum up, policies in eastern Germany are beginning to show results. A substantial part of the economy has already been transferred to the private sector and there are increasing signs of a recovery in production. However, the costs in terms of employment losses in the east and in deteriorating public finances have been high. Efforts to force too rapid a pace of wage catch-up, prompted by optimistic expectations of the speed of convergence, have been a major factor behind the size of employment losses. The sheer size of investment promotion and of employment protection and creation measures is bound to have some unavoidable distortionary effects on competition and the development of the private sector. These effects should be carefully monitored and social-support and labour-market schemes need increasingly to be designed so as to minimise such interference. While temporary high public borrowing has been acceptable in view of the exceptional circumstances, it should now be brought down progressively as is, indeed, intended by the Government also with a view to paving the way for easier monetary conditions. Against a background of medium-term fiscal consolidation and attention to the microeconomic effects of convergence-promoting policies, progress towards full integration of the two parts of Germany may take longer than widely thought at the start of the unification process, but it is important that it be built on sound foundations.

Notes and references

1. For a detailed discussion of the events which led to the unification of Germany and of the problems resulting from the "generous" conversion rate of the East German mark and the wholesale take-over of western Germany's legal and institutional framework see OECD, *Economic Survey of Germany,* 1990 and 1991.

2. See OECD, *Economic Survey of Germany,* 1991, p. 116 *et seq.*.

3. Economic and institutional integration of the two parts of Germany is progressing fast, as evidenced by the huge flows of goods, services, capital and labour between the two regions. However, there are still severe statistical problems in presenting a reliable picture of macroeconomic developments in the eastern Länder so that for many economic variables aggregation is difficult or not feasible. More importantly, the forces shaping economic developments in the old and new Länder are still so diverse that a combined analysis of economic trends and prospects make little sense. However, whenever appropriate, references are made to all-German developments.

4. According to estimates by the five major economic institutes GNP plunged by some 30 per cent after a drop of perhaps half that size in 1990, see e.g. Ifo-Institut (1992), "Die Lage der Weltwirtschaft und der deutschen Wirtschaft im Frühjahr 1992", *Ifo-Wirtschaftskonjunktur,* 4/1992.

5. Compensation per employee rose about 25 per cent, dependent employment fell some 20 per cent and the consumption deflator rose by almost 15 per cent.

6. Social transfers to eastern German households are estimated to have been close to DM 75 billion, corresponding to more than a third of disposable income.

7. Private investment is mainly being furthered through four programmes: the investment premium scheme, running for two years (1991 and 1992); ERP (European Recovery Programme – the Marshall Plan) credits; the regional subsidisation scheme; and the own-capital credit programme. In 1991, DM 4$\frac{1}{2}$ billion tax subsidies were given and DM 21 billion of subsidised loans were granted.

8. Income from entrepreneurship and property in the fourth quarter of 1991 was some 4$\frac{1}{4}$ per cent lower than a year earlier.

9. From the second to the fourth quarter of 1991, gross fixed investment spending fell at an annual rate of 10 per cent.

10. Exports of investment goods constitute more than half of western German exports.

11. For a fuller discussion of trade developments and export performance, see section on balance of payments below.

12. As noted above, GNP rose 0.3 points less fast, the main reason being that it excludes dependent income earned by non-residents, including eastern Germans who work in western Germany but live in the east (the so-called *Pendler* – see box).

13. The relevant employment concept for GDP-based productivity calculations is *domestic employment*, which covers all individuals working in western Germany irrespective of whether they are residents or not.

14. The stock of unemployed ethnic Germans (Aussiedler) by the end of 1991 was around 140 000 persons, some 20 000 lower than a year before. See Federal Labour Office, *Amtliche Nachrichten,* February 1992.

15. Foreign workers also gained from the employment boom, however, at a declining rate. Except for 1989, the inflow of this category of labour was higher than absorption.

16. See Klös (1991), "Zuwanderungsbedingter Potentialzuwachs: Substitution Arbeitsloser oder Mehrbeschäftigung?'' in *IW-Trends* 3/91 pp. A-24 to A-49.

17. Employment had already fallen by almost 1 million from mid-1989 to mid-1990 due to emigration.

18. See DIW, *Wochenbericht,* 3/92 and 5-6/92.

19. For a brief explanation of the coverage and differences between financial balances on a national-accounts and financial-statistics basis, see below.

20. The fund manages liabilities taken over from the former GDR public institutions.

21. With 1.6 million full-time employed in the public sector for 16 million inhabitants (or one in ten) in the east against a corresponding ratio of one to sixteen in the west, there would seem to be a considerable "administrative overhang" in the new Länder.

22. Relative to the budget for 1991, the envisaged rise in spending is just below 3 per cent, consistent with the guideline of the Financial Planning Council.

23. Data in this section are calculated by the Bundesbank. They deviate from budget data by incorporating credits from specialised credit institutions, tax exemptions and interest payments. See *Bundesbank Monthly Report,* March, 1992.

24. This should not be taken as a measure of the costs to the public sector of unification: part of the expenditure consists of credits which should be repaid; benefits also accrue from lower division-related costs, and from the spill-over effects from eastern German demand on incomes and hence tax revenues in western Germany.

25. Debt servicing of the fund's borrowing – rising from DM 2 billion in 1991 to DM 9½ billion by 1995 – is shared equally between the federal and the old Länder governments.

26. As public financial support only covers a part of the entire financing needs, the supported volume of private investments was considerably larger.

27. The Unity Fund ("Fonds Deutsche Einheit"), the European Recovery Programme fund, the Burden-equalisation fund ("Lastenausgleichsfonds") and the Debt-management fund ("Kreditabwicklungsfonds").

28. See OECD (1991), *op. cit.,* p. 70 ff.

29. In particular, the law regulating compensation for earlier (1945-1949) expropriation may constitute a severe burden for federal finances.

30. Outstanding Hermes credits reportedly attained DM 30 billion by the end of 1991. Against a backlog of DM 70 billion pending applications, a ceiling of DM 5 billion for new guarantees was imposed for 1992.

31. The average conversion rate applied to the former GDR financial balances was 1.8, which was expected to increase the all-German money supply in line with the (then) estimated GNP for the eastern Länder. In the event, M3 exceeded the planned level by about 5 per cent, and when the monetary statistics of the two parts of Germany were combined (from January 1991), the all-German M3 exceeded western German M3 of a year earlier by about 20 per cent. About 10 percentage points could be arithmetically accounted for by the extension of the currency area and a further 5 percentage points by one year's monetary growth in line with nominal potential GNP and the trend decline in velocity. The remaining 5 percentage points could then be considered as excess liquidity created in the wake of currency union in eastern and western Germany.

32. The demand for currency was boosted by prospects of the reintroduction of a withholding tax on interest income, and the increased use of the Deutschemark as a parallel currency in the eastern European countries.

33. The Government plans to introduce a 25 per cent tax withholding on interest income above tax allowances, which at the same time will be increased tenfold. It is estimated that more than 80 per cent of private households will be exempt from taxes on their interest income. Foreign investors will generally be exempt from the new withholding tax.

34. See OECD (1991), *op. cit.,* p. 94 ff.

35. The Treuhandanstalt's guidelines for the privatisation of enterprises state, *inter alia,* that account should be taken of the following: the continued operation and modernisation of the business by the purchaser; securing employment; consideration of the survivability of suppliers from eastern Germany; the contribution to the strength of the area around the enterprise, and the possible future contribution to tax incomes. See Carlin, W. and C. Mayer (1992), ''The Treuhandanstalt: Privatisation by State and Market'', unpublished NBER conference paper, pp.16-17.

36. Carlin and Mayer (1992), *op. cit.,* note that proceeds from sales per guaranteed job declined from DM 23 000 to DM 16 000 between the first and the second half of 1991 and that over the same period, investment guarantees per job rose from DM 75 000 to DM 115 000.

37. In the Ifo survey referred to above, industrial firms expect a turnaround in export sales from a 1 per cent fall in 1991 to a 7 per cent rise in 1992.

38. See OECD, *Economic Survey of Germany* 1990/91, pp. 19-20.

39. Non-union members are always covered *de jure* by the contracts covering their respective enterprises, if the employer is a member of the organisation that negotiated the agreement.

40. Unions in Germany are organised on a ''federal'' basis, with one main umbrella organisation, the DGB (*Deutscher Gewerkschaftsbund*), covering the whole economy, which is divided into sixteen unions covering each major industrial sector (thus IG-Metall, IG- , etc.), which in turn are organised regionally. There are also separate union organisations (one for civil

servants, one for white-collar workers, and the Christian union) but these play little part in wage bargaining. The employers' organisations are grouped under the BDA (*Bundesvereinigung der Deutschen Arbeitgeberverbände*) which has around 45 member associations, comprising roughly 300 local organisations, while the public sector is organised in a joint association. There are a few exceptions to regional bargaining, where a particular employer is large and homogeneous enough to warrant a separate contract; thus Volkswagen conducts negotiations on its own, without the intermediation of an employers' organisation.

41. Some 40 per cent of all wage settlements consist of agreeing to implement settlements already reached for other groups of workers. In addition, there are nation-wide agreements for public-sector employees, the transport, banking, insurance and some smaller sectors.

42. Job classification schemes cover virtually all grades of employee; they are defined regionally, but are generally comparable across regions.

43. See OECD, *Employment Outlook,* 1991, table 4.1.

44. Co-determination through the *Betriebsrat* covers working hour arrangements, modes of wage payment, holiday schedules, measurement of performance, safety at work, fringe benefits, special premiums and piece-work rates, appointments and dismissals.

45. Labour courts rule, for example, on disputes arising from *Tarif* or individual employment contracts, claims arising from illegal strike activity, employees' intellectual property rights, offences against the Company Constitution Law and on union bargaining rights. Their jurisdiction does not extend to civil servants.

46. In addition the relevant umbrella organisations on the union and employers' sides must give their consent.

47. These provisions may, of course, affect firms' total costs.

48. Overall, about 2½ per cent of all employees – about one million – are covered by declarations on wages.

49. See, for example, Steedman H., Mason G. and Wagner K., "Intermediate skills in the workplace: deployment, standards and supply in Britain, France and Germany," in the *National Institute Economic Review,* London, May 1991. The authors note that among technicians and foremen in western Germany in 1987, less than 8 per cent were without a vocational qualification, whereas the corresponding figures for Britain and France ranged from 27 to 55 per cent (*op. cit.,* page 64). For a discussion of skill levels in eastern Germany relative to those in western Germany see OECD, *Economic Survey of Germany,* 1990/91.

50. There are some 1½ million apprentices in western Germany and a similar number of 15 to 21 year-olds receives full-time education. In the same age-group, around 1 million have full-time jobs (other than apprentices).

51. In the case of the long-term (at least one year) unemployed the subsidy may amount to up to 80 per cent of wages for the first six months and up to 60 per cent for the following six months, in both western and eastern Germany.

52. The Federal Labour Office (Bundesanstalt für Arbeit) was set up in 1952 as a self-governing, non-profit organisation whose board is composed of members from employers and trade union organisations and all (federal, Länder and municipal) levels of government. It runs 184 local offices (of which 38 are in the new Länder).

53. Labour market laws forbid profits being made from intermediation in the labour market, with the exceptions mentioned.

54. In April 1991 the EC court found the monopoly inconsistent with the EC treaty in the case of executive recruitment agencies; the case in question did not require a ruling on the more general application of the monopoly. In March 1992 the German federal court for social security matters found the monopoly consistent with both the EC treaty and the German constitution.

55. In fact, only some 20 per cent of all job placements are mediated through agencies of the Labour Office; however, 50 per cent of jobs found by the unemployed follow this route. These figures are relatively high by in comparison with many countries. See Walwei U. "Monopoly or coexistence – placement services and the future of the labour market," 1992.

56. See OECD, *Economic Survey of Italy,* 1990/91, pp. 51-52.

57. These are the Company Constitution Law "Betriebsverfassungsgesetz", the Dismissal Protection Law "Kündigungsschutzgesetz" and the General Law of the People "Bürgerliches Gesetzbuch".

58. By dismissing single people without dependents before those with children, for example.

59. Büchtemann C., (1989) *Befristete Arbeitsverträge nach dem Beschäftigungsförderungsgesetz (Besch FG 1985). Ergebnisse einer empirischen Untersuchung in Auftrag des Bundesministeriums für Arbeit und Sozialordnung,* Bonn.

60. OECD, *Employment Outlook,* 1991, chapter 7. The nominal replacement ratio is 63 or 68 per cent of monthly earnings, according to family status. The OECD calculations provided international comparability by adjusting for extra holiday payments etc. not included in normal monthly wage and salary payments.

61. For single people. For couples Germany ranked second.

62. The period of entitlement to unemployment insurance benefits depends on the length of time during which contributions have been paid and the age of the unemployed person. The average entitlement period is about one year; in some cases, in particular for older people, entitlement can last for up to 32 months.

63. See, for example, Chapter I of the *Economic Survey of Germany,* 1990/1991, OECD, July 1991.

64. Such a choice has not been available in other eastern European countries attempting the transition to a market economy. Whether the ability to cushion the adjustment turns out to be an advantage (through reducing the immediate pain and hence allowing it to proceed faster) or a disadvantage (by reducing its urgency and hence protracting adjustment) in the medium term remains to be seen. The length of time that convergence may take remains a major imponderable. It is unlikely that it will proceed uniformly, and complete convergence in terms of statistical averages will never occur and is not a useful objective: some eastern German areas may become richer than parts of western Germany while others remain behind; after all, slowly changing regional differences persist in western Germany.

65. Particularly in areas which are relatively highly regulated, such as telecommunications, or potentially environmentally sensitive, such as new road construction.

66. Whether labour intensive methods are automatically low-technology is a moot – perhaps semantic – point. It is not the level of technology but the quantity (or, rather, value) of capital equipment which is low, while the required skill level may even be higher in some cases. Needless to say, high wages are preferable to low wages if the level of employment is not an issue.

67. A survey taken soon after reunification – and hence before open unemployment had risen very far – showed that eastern Germans thought they were more likely to move to get a job than simply to increase their earnings; see Akerlof, G., Rose, A.K., Yellen, J.L. and Hessemius, H. (1991) "East Germany in from the cold: the economic aftermath of currency union," Brookings, Washington. See also Walsh, B.M. (1974) "Expectations, information and human migration: specifying an econometric model of Irish migration to Britain" *Journal of Regional Science* no. 14, where unemployment differentials were found to play an equally important role with wage differentials in explaining (net) migration between Britain and Ireland, where linguistic and institutional barriers are probably no higher than between the formerly divided parts of Germany.

68. The notion that workers in any labour market have the ability to "offer' themselves at low wages is probably inappropriate anyway; there is usually a 'going wage" if only at a local or firm level. But the point remains that in western Germany *employers'* ability to take advantage of potential employees *willingness* to accept lower wages is severely restricted.

69. Although it has been difficult to establish a stable econometric relation between unemployment and wage behaviour, comparisons with other OECD countries suggest that wages in Germany have been relatively unresponsive to unemployment but relatively responsive to prices, implying a considerable degree of overall real wage rigidity (see OECD, *Economies in Transition,* 1989). At a regional level it has been observed that regional variation in wage levels tends to be positively correlated with variation in unemployment levels, and that regional wage differentials do not tend to change over time in response to unemployment differentials. See Paqué, K., (1991) "Structural rigidity in West Germany 1950-89. Some new econometric evidence", *Kiel Working Paper* no. 489.

70. See Paqué, *op. cit.*.

71. To some extent local bargaining following the *Tarif* agreements may offset this tendency. Inter-industry differentials may have increased over the last three decades, however; see Holmlund B., Zetterberg J., (1991) "Insiders and outsiders in wage determination. Evidence from five countries" *European Economic Review* no. 35.

72. It also appears to vary substantially by size of firm. In 1988, average labour costs (which includes non-wage costs and employers' contributions to social security etc.) were up to 40 per cent higher in firms with more than 1 000 employees than in those with 10 to 100 employees (see 1991 *Statistical Handbook,* page 577, table 22.10.2). This comparison is not corrected for differences in the age and qualification structure of the labour force, but is nevertheless indicative of some considerable degree of variation in effective wages.

73. See Paqué, *op. cit.*. Paqué concludes that both effective and *Tarif* wages are inflexible, but the former somewhat less than the latter.

74.	Both managers and employees in weak firms, where the risk of redundancy was high even with "responsible" behaviour, shared an interest in opting for high wage settlements in order to exploit the unemployment benefit system's link of benefit payments to latest earnings.

75.	Union representatives often justify this position by saying that firms which are in difficulties are there because management has made mistakes, and that workers should not be made to "pay" for these mistakes with lower wages. This would normally have the result of transferring the risk from wage levels to employment levels; since reducing the workforce has significant costs both in monetary terms (because of the requirement for a social plan) and in terms of efficiency (firms are not always free to dismiss the least efficient of their workforce) the natural result is a very conservative hiring policy, and in the long run a tendency to go for a more labour-saving technology than would otherwise be desired.

76.	The catch-up settlements do, however, include clauses providing for renegotiation in the event that productivity converge faster than expected. It is now being suggested that these clauses be used to reduce the rate of wage catch-up. Such renegotiation could be expected to lower the rate of job losses and improve the budgetary position.

77.	Estimates from DIW of wage costs by industry during 1991 show that on average unit labour costs were no higher at the end of the year than at the beginning. This, however, is only after massive job-losses, and may take insufficient account of subsidies (see below).

78.	An interesting recent settlement covers the printing industry. 100 per cent catch-up is specified for 1995, except that if economic conditions are particularly poor, this may be reduced to 85 per cent.

79.	Known as *Investivlohn*.

80.	In addition, average wages tend to be higher in firms still owned by the Treuhandanstalt than in already privatised firms. While this may be a result of indirect wage-subsidisation, the evidence is not conclusive since industrial and skill structure may play a significant role.

81.	See Buttler F. (1991), "Der Arbeitsmarkt in den neuen Bundesländern 1991/92", *Mitteilungen aus der Arbeitsmarkt- und Berufsforschung, 1991, no. 4.*

82.	Formally, a *Beschäftigungsgesellschaft* should be set up as an independent company, primarily aiming to create employment and/or offer training, and is then eligible for funding from the employment-creation programme of the Labour Office. It may offer only fixed-term contracts (for Labour-Office-funded jobs, up to two years). The very large companies may serve only public sector contracts.

83.	Institut für Arbeitsmarkt- und Berufsforschung der Bundesanstalt für Arbeit, "Kurzbericht", 7 November 1991, page 3.

84.	In fact, the basic contractual (Tarif) wages are paid. As discussed elsewhere, most western German companies pay more than the (western German) Tarif rates; but in eastern Germany a new company might not be in a position to pay higher rates.

85.	Although employment in the employment companies is restricted to fixed-term contracts, it may still offer greater security under current circumstances than jobs in the private sector. Specific contracts between the Labour Office and employment agencies have a maximum duration of one year, however.

Annex

Chronology of main economic events

1991

January

The abolition of the stock exchange transactions tax, announced at the beginning of 1990, comes into force.

The Government announces that social security contributions will be increased by 2½ percentage points as from 1 April 1991, as part of measures to save DM 35 billion in the 1991 budget.

The Bundesbank raises both the discount rate and the Lombard rate by half a point, to 6.5 and 9.0 per cent, respectively.

February

The Government confirms the target for federal government borrowing in 1991, at DM 70½ billion. Total expenditure is to be DM 400 billion. The aims of the financial plan for 1991-94 announced in November are also reaffirmed.

March

The Bundestag adopts the Act Removing Impediments to the Privatisation of Companies and Promoting Investment (*Gesetz zur Beseitigung von Hemmnissen bei der Privatisierung von Unternehmen und zur Förderung von Investoren*). The Act primarily aims at creating the legal framework conditions for selling property to investors rather than giving it back to former owners and at more rapidly settling ownership claims in the new Länder.

The Federal Government adopts the joint Federal Government/Länder project Upswing East (*Gemeinschaftswerk Aufschwung-Ost*). It provides for additional funds for specific measures in the new Länder amounting to DM 12 billion in both 1991 and 1992. This includes funds for local infrastructure, transport infrastructure, housing, urban development, training measures and job creation schemes, extension of investment grants and immediate support in the environmental field.

April

The government coalition adopts supplementary tax benefits in the housing sector of the new Länder.

May

The Deregulation Commission submits its final report. A working group of the government parties discusses on the basis of this report which further deregulation measures to take in the fields of insurances, transport, electricity, technical assessments and expert reports, markets for legal and economic consultancy, the crafts and the labour market.

June

The Bundestag adopts the 1991 Federal Budget. Budgeted expenditure amounts to DM 410.3 billion. Net borrowing is fixed at DM 66.4 billion.

The splitting and privatisation of the retail trade in eastern Germany was completed.

July

To cover additional spending in the new Länder, the following tax increases enter into force within the framework of the Solidarity Act (*Solidaritätsgesetz*):
- a surcharge on personal and corporate income tax (solidarity contribution) amounting to 7.5 per cent of the tax due as of 1 July 1991 and limited to one year;
- an increase in the mineral oil tax by an average of 25 per cent;
- an increase in the insurance tax from 7 per cent to 10 per cent on the taxable insurance premiums;
- an increase in the tobacco tax as of 1 March 1992.

The 1991 Tax Amendment Act (*Steueränderungsgesetz*) enters into force. It aims at promoting investment and creating new jobs in the new Länder and at amending tax legislation and other stipulations: abolishing special support for Berlin and the former inner German border regions; special write-off possibilities of up to 50 per cent of plant and equipment expenditure and costs for company buildings as of 1991.

The Bundesbank lowers the money supply M3 target range from 4 to 6 per cent to 3 to 5 per cent.

The Federal Government submits the medium-term financial plan for the 1991-1995 period. It is planned to raise expenditure until 1995 by an annual average of 2.3 per cent and reduce net borrowing to less than DM 50 billion in 1992 and to DM 25 billion in 1995.

The Federal government announces plans to cut subsidies by DM 32 billion in the 1992-1994 period, relative to existing projections.

Old-age pensions are raised by 15 per cent in the new Länder and by 4.7 per cent in the old Länder.

August

The *Bundesbank* raises the discount rate from 6.5 per cent to 7.5 per cent and the Lombard rate from 9 per cent to 9.25 per cent.

October

The first stage of the housing rent reform in the new Länder enters into force: It allows landlords to double the basic rents, which had been constant since the 1930s, from an average of DM 1 to DM 2 per square metre. Along with changes in other costs, this makes for a rise in rents of more than 300 per cent.

December

The money supply target for 1992 is announced as a range of 3.5 to 5.5 per cent.

The Bundesbank raises the discount rate from 7.5 per cent to 8 per cent and the Lombard rate from 9.25 per cent to 9.75 per cent.

The Bundestag adopts the 1991 supplementary budget amounting to DM 6.3 billion. Additional expenditure is financed by means of budgetary shifts and by expenditure cuts.

The Bundestag adopts the 1992 Federal budget. The budget volume amounts to DM 422.1 billion. Net borrowing is planned to amount to DM 45.3 billion.

1992

January

In the new Länder, old-age pensions are raised by 11.65 per cent. Furthermore, the Pensions Conversion Act (*Rentenüberleitungsgesetz*) brings western German legislation into force for pensions in the new Länder.

February

The 1992 Tax Amendment Act enters into force. It contains financial improvements for families, tax relief for industry and the abolition of a number of tax benefits as of 1 January 1992 as well as the increase in the value-added tax rate from 14 per cent to 15 per cent as of 1 January 1993 (the reduced tax rate, e.g. for food, remains unchanged).

STATISTICAL AND STRUCTURAL ANNEX

Table A. **Selected background statistics**

	1982	1983	1984	1985	1986	1987	1988	1989	1990	1991
A. Percentage change from previous year at constant prices										
Private consumption	-1.5	1.3	1.6	1.5	3.4	3.3	2.7	1.7	4.7	2.5
Gross fixed investment	-5.3	3.3	0.3	0.0	3.6	2.1	4.6	7.0	8.8	6.7
Construction	-4.0	1.6	1.1	-5.8	3.1	0.0	3.1	4.8	5.3	4.1
Public	-8.9	-8.0	-2.0	0.6	8.2	0.0	0.3	4.3	2.1	0.7
Residential	-4.9	5.7	2.0	-10.0	-0.6	-1.2	3.7	4.8	7.8	4.3
Business	-4.5	4.9	-0.1	5.5	4.6	4.0	5.9	8.5	10.5	8.6
Machinery and equipment	-7.2	6.0	-0.9	9.0	4.2	4.9	6.6	9.8	12.9	9.4
GNP at market prices	-1.1	1.9	3.1	1.8	2.2	1.5	3.7	3.8	4.5	3.1
GNP implicit price deflator	4.5	3.4	2.1	2.2	3.3	1.9	1.5	2.6	3.4	4.6
Industrial production	-3.0	2.2	2.9	5.0	1.9	0.4	3.6	4.8	5.2	3.0
Employment	-1.2	-1.4	0.2	0.7	1.4	0.7	0.8	1.4	2.9	2.7
Compensation of employees (current prices)	3.1	2.1	3.7	3.9	5.2	4.2	4.0	4.5	7.5	7.9
Productivity (GNP/employment)	-0.5	3.1	3.3	1.0	0.8	0.7	2.9	2.4	1.9	1.6
Unit labour costs (compensation of employees/ GNP)	4.2	0.2	0.6	2.0	2.9	2.7	0.3	0.7	2.9	4.6
B. Percentage ratios										
Gross fixed investment										
As a per cent of GNP at constant prices	20.0	20.3	19.7	19.4	19.7	19.8	20.0	20.6	21.4	22.2
Stockbuilding										
As a per cent of GNP at constant prices	-0.7	0.0	0.4	0.1	0.1	0.1	0.6	1.1	0.5	0.5
Foreign balance										
As a per cent of GNP at constant prices	2.6	2.2	3.3	4.1	3.0	2.0	2.0	3.1	3.1	3.2
Compensation of employees										
As a per cent of GNP at current prices	58.7	56.9	56.1	56.0	55.8	56.2	55.5	54.4	54.2	54.2
Direct taxes										
As a per cent of household income	10.5	10.4	10.4	10.7	10.6	10.8	10.7	11.2	10.1	10.8
Household saving										
As a per cent of disposable income	12.7	10.9	11.4	11.4	12.3	12.6	12.8	12.5	13.9	13.7
Unemployment										
As a per cent of civilian labour force	5.0	6.6	7.1	7.1	6.4	6.2	6.2	5.6	4.9	4.3
C. Other indicator										
Current balance (billion $)	5.1	5.3	9.8	16.4	39.5	45.7	50.5	57.2	47.9	-20.7

Sources: Statistisches Bundesamt, *Volkswirtschaftliche Gesamtrechnungen*, Reihe 1; Deutsche Bundesbank, *Statistische Beihefte zu den Monatsberichten*, Reihe 4.

Table B. Gross domestic product by origin

DM billion

	1983	1984	1985	1986	1987	1988	1989	1990	1991 Western Germany	1991 Eastern Germany	1991 Germany
Current prices											
Agriculture, forestry, fishing	33.23	34.46	31.92	34.0	30.24	33.72	37.97	38.35	32.18	3.3	35.5
Mining and quarrying, energy	61.25	63.98	66.53	65.91	68.67	67.84	69.72	71.59	73.98	67.5	1 067.3
Manufacturing	519.42	542.60	578.85	620.44	624.69	652.67	689.61	740.18	780.33	⎱	⎱
Construction	99.05	99.72	94.81	100.13	101.68	106.25	114.34	129.71	145.47	..	..
Trade, transport, communications	241.64	256.04	261.46	269.58	279.54	294.66	311.07	333.14	359.20	35.1	392.3
Government[1]	195.74	199.95	207.26	217.12	225.82	231.86	238.46	252.77	271.16	44.8	382.3
Non-profit organisations, households	38.10	39.99	42.68	46.42	49.28	51.67	53.93	58.35	64.29	..	..
Other services	480.11	514.15	539.67	571.69	610.56	657.31	705.78	779.00	872.70	99.8	972.5
Gross domestic product at market prices	1 668.54	1 750.89	1 823.18	1 925.29	1 990.48	2 095.98	2 220.88	2 403.09	2 599.31	183.0	2 782.3
1985 prices											
Agriculture, forestry, fishing	32.10	34.11	31.92	35.25	32.12	34.48	35.25	37.58	34.22	..	..
Mining and quarrying, energy	64.03	65.19	66.53	65.83	68.81	68.35	71.41	72.40	72.782	..	..
Manufacturing	543.60	559.52	578.85	587.02	575.59	593.76	616.05	644.57	661.802	..	..
Construction	100.02	100.39	94.81	96.22	94.54	96.43	99.67	104.05	106.922	..	..
Trade, transport, communications	246.77	256.97	261.46	264.84	271.83	285.32	297.25	314.0	329.282	..	..
Government[1]	202.11	204.34	207.26	210.09	212.79	215.22	215.59	219.12	222.652	..	..
Non-profit organisations, households	40.04	41.17	42.68	44.49	45.85	47.24	48.59	50.63	52.872	..	..
Other services	512.23	527.66	539.67	560.03	588.75	619.71	640.35	676.07	710.532	..	..
Gross domestic product at market prices	1 740.90	1 789.35	1 823.18	1 863.77	1 890.28	1 960.51	2 024.16	2 118.42	2 191.05	..	..

1. Central and local government, municipalities and social security.
Source: Statistisches Bundesamt, *Volkswirtschaftliche Gesamtrechnungen*, Fachserie 18, Reihe 1.

Table C. Gross national product by demand components
DM billion

	1983	1984	1985	1986	1987	1988	1989	1990	1991 Western Germany	1991 Eastern Germany	1991 Germany
Current prices											
Private consumption	959.28	1 001.20	1 036.53	1 066.43	1 108.02	1 153.69	1 209.57	1 299.23	1 379.10	196.3	1 575.4
Public consumption	336.44	350.44	365.72	382.55	397.28	412.38	418.78	443.08	469.38	90.2	559.6
Gross fixed investment	340.81	350.67	355.81	373.48	385.78	409.90	451.40	509.51	569.72	72.4	642.1
Machinery and equipment	134.95	137.13	153.03	160.87	169.43	182.46	204.87	234.52	263.76	36.0	299.8
Public	4.66	5.11	5.95	6.54	7.09	7.18	8.21	9.09	9.41	..	..
Private	130.29	132.02	147.08	154.33	162.34	175.28	196.66	225.43	254.35	..	..
Construction	205.86	213.54	202.78	212.61	216.35	227.44	246.53	274.99	305.96	36.4	342.4
Public	37.52	37.05	36.96	40.75	40.90	41.73	44.32	47.44	51.21	..	..
Residential	105.77	111.04	100.85	101.83	102.58	108.61	117.90	134.64	150.41	..	..
Other private	62.57	65.45	64.97	70.03	72.87	77.10	84.31	92.91	104.34	..	..
Stockbuilding	-1.50	5.32	1.25	2.92	-0.56	10.30	20.71	8.13	9.06	2.4	11.5
Total domestic demand	1 635.03	1 707.63	1 759.31	1 825.38	1 890.52	1 986.27	2 100.46	2 259.95	2 427.26	361.3	2 788.6
Exports of goods and services	522.24	585.80	644.66	637.02	637.52	687.87	787.94	881.76	1 009.08	59.2	824.0
Imports of goods and services	481.57	530.13	569.47	526.30	525.04	566.14	643.20	716.21	821.14	227.3	804.1
Gross national product at market prices	1 675.70	1 763.30	1 834.50	1 936.10	2 003.00	2 108.00	2 245.20	2 425.50	2 615.20	193.2	2 808.5
1985 prices											
Private consumption	1 005.92	1 021.68	1 036.53	1 072.01	1 106.88	1 137.0	1 156.73	1 211.12	1 241.03	..	..
Public consumption	349.54	358.31	365.72	375.04	380.85	389.10	382.64	390.51	393.54	..	..
Gross fixed investment	354.59	355.70	355.81	368.49	376.22	393.68	421.38	458.64	489.16	..	..
Machinery and equipment	141.64	140.36	153.03	159.46	167.25	178.27	195.69	220.93	241.73	..	..
Public	4.89	5.22	5.95	6.48	6.99	6.96	7.73	8.43	8.46	..	..
Private	136.75	135.14	147.08	152.98	160.26	171.31	187.96	212.50	233.27	..	..
Construction	212.95	215.34	202.78	209.03	208.97	215.41	225.69	237.71	247.43	..	..
Public	38.61	37.42	36.96	39.93	39.43	39.59	40.83	41.14	41.47	..	..
Residential	109.79	112.0	100.85	100.27	99.02	102.70	107.60	115.94	120.87	..	..
Other private	64.55	65.92	64.97	68.83	70.52	73.12	77.26	80.63	85.09	..	..
Stockbuilding	0.52	7.47	1.25	2.69	1.0	12.03	21.89	11.74	11.06	..	..
Total domestic demand	1 710.57	1 743.16	1 759.31	1 818.23	1 864.95	1 931.81	1 982.64	2 072.01	2 134.79	..	..
Exports of goods and services	554.12	601.64	644.66	645.24	651.31	689.62	768.27	852.59	955.75	..	..
Imports of goods and services	516.29	542.80	569.47	589.07	613.96	649.63	704.11	785.90	884.64	..	..
Gross national product at market prices	1 748.40	1 802.00	1 834.50	1 874.40	1 902.30	1 971.80	2 046.80	2 138.70	2 205.90	..	..

Source: Statistisches Bundesamt, *Volkswirtschaftliche Gesamtrechnungen*, Fachserie 18, Reihe 1.

Table D. Distribution of national income
DM billion, current prices

	1981	1982	1983	1984	1985	1986	1987	1988	1989	1990	1991[1]
Compensation of employees	905.98	933.93	953.44	988.33	1 026.41	1 079.49	1 124.70	1 169.38	1 221.89	1 313.52	1 417.36
less:											
Employers' social security contributions	162.09	169.49	176.02	185.40	192.63	202.86	211.89	220.51	229.11	244.03	263.15
Employees' social security contributions	97.33	102.22	105.49	111.08	117.29	124.22	129.33	135.60	142.13	152.56	168.80
Wage tax	116.72	122.24	127.35	135.45	145.52	150.01	162.36	165.48	179.17	173.63	206.73
Net wages and salaries[2]	529.84	539.98	544.58	556.40	570.97	602.40	621.12	647.79	671.48	743.44	778.68
Income from property and entrepreneurship	273.83	280.25	324.66	358.80	380.36	418.06	425.30	466.16	512.43	557.46	578.87
less:											
Direct taxes on business and property income	59.38	58.58	59.06	62.62	71.24	73.56	69.30	75.86	90.09	83.93	94.78
Net income from property and entrepreneurship	214.45	221.67	265.60	296.18	309.12	344.50	356.00	390.30	422.34	473.73	484.09
of which:											
Retained profits	−23.96	−22.33	10.18	3.01	−2.38	33.22	35.64	64.80	61.84	7.0	68.59
Accruing to Government	−14.71	−13.83	−19.36	−20.71	−20.53	−23.30	−30.74	−39.92	−28.89	−29.71	−40.34
Distributed to households	253.12	257.83	274.78	313.88	332.03	334.58	351.10	365.42	389.39	426.44	455.84
Gross national income	1 179.81	1 214.18	1 278.10	1 347.13	1 406.77	1 497.55	1 550.00	1 635.54	1 734.32	1 871.58	1 996.23
Memorandum items:											
Household disposable income	1 022.42	1 049.73	1 076.67	1 129.84	1 170.11	1 215.70	1 267.58	1 323.15	1 382.95	1 507.81	1 597.71
Household saving ratio[3]	13.6	12.7	10.9	11.4	11.4	12.3	12.6	12.8	12.5	13.9	13.7

1. Western Germany only.
2. Including voluntary fringe benefits.
3. Per cent of household disposable income.
Source: Statistisches Bundesamt, *Volkswirtschaftliche Gesamtrechnungen,* Fachserie 18, Reihe 1.

110

Table E. **Receipts and expenditure of general government: national accounts basis**

DM billion, current prices

	1982	1983	1984	1985	1986	1987	1988	1989	1990	1991[1]
Current receipts										
Income from property and entrepreneurship	30.20	30.73	32.01	34.74	33.88	27.04	19.89	31.29	33.75	34.26
Indirect taxes	201.89	214.39	226.13	230.31	236.17	245.50	257.11	278.27	303.0	340.30
Direct taxes	193.18	200.36	213.02	229.64	237.04	245.94	255.41	281.78	270.88	315.33
Social security contributions	284.48	290.34	304.58	320.11	337.40	350.55	366.52	383.31	410.59	448.28
Other current transfers received	16.27	19.52	20.61	20.59	22.85	22.27	25.53	24.94	26.03	31.92
Total current receipts	726.02	755.34	796.35	835.39	867.34	891.30	924.46	999.59	1 044.25	1 170.09
Current expenditure										
Final consumption expenditure	326.19	336.44	350.44	365.72	382.55	397.28	412.38	418.78	443.08	469.38
Wages and salaries	178.07	183.37	187.01	193.88	203.30	211.50	216.92	222.64	235.88	252.86
Goods and services	148.12	153.07	163.43	171.84	179.25	185.78	195.46	196.14	207.20	216.52
Subsidies	29.42	31.72	36.33	37.94	41.31	44.80	47.74	46.80	48.77	48.55
Debt-interest payments	44.03	50.09	52.72	55.27	57.18	57.78	59.81	60.18	63.46	74.60
Current transfers paid	319.75	325.91	334.67	342.04	353.85	371.39	392.53	408.24	469.89	573.33
Total current expenditure	719.39	744.16	774.16	800.97	834.89	871.25	912.46	934.0	1 025.20	1 165.86
Savings	6.63	11.18	22.19	34.42	32.45	20.05	12.00	65.59	19.05	4.23
Depreciation	11.27	12.12	12.68	13.12	13.57	14.07	14.69	15.57	16.64	18.05
Net capital transfers received	−25.12	−23.72	−26.69	−25.72	−24.13	−23.97	−23.02	−24.42	−25.41	−43.50
Gross fixed investment	45.26	42.18	42.16	42.91	47.29	47.99	48.91	52.53	56.53	60.62
Financial balance (net lending)	−52.48	−42.60	−33.98	−21.09	−25.40	−37.84	−45.24	4.21	−46.25	−81.84
As a per cent of GNP	−3.3	−2.5	−1.9	−1.1	−1.3	−1.9	−2.1	0.2	−1.9	−3.1

1. All Germany.
Source: Statistisches Bundesamt, *Volkswirtschaftliche Gesamtrechnungen*, Fachserie 18, Reihe 1.

Table F. **Balance of payments**
DM billion

	1982	1983	1984	1985	1986	1987	1988	1989	1990	1991
A. Current account										
1. Foreign trade, net	51.2	42.1	54.0	73.4	112.6	117.7	128.0	134.6	105.4	21.9
Exports (f.o.b)	427.7	432.3	488.2	537.2	526.4	527.4	567.7	641.0	662.0	665.8
Imports (c.i.f)	376.5	390.2	434.3	463.8	413.7	409.6	439.6	506.5	556.7	643.9
2. Supplementary trade items	0.8	3.3	-1.1	-1.3	-1.5	-1.1	1.1	-1.3	-0.5	1.8
Balance of trade	52.0	45.4	52.9	72.0	111.2	116.6	129.2	133.3	104.9	23.7
3. Services, net	-13.7	-6.6	4.7	5.4	1.7	-5.0	-8.4	8.4	7.9	2.6
Receipts	118.6	120.7	135.4	144.3	143.6	146.6	154.7	190.5	214.6	235.4
Expenditure	132.3	127.3	130.6	138.9	141.9	151.6	163.1	182.1	206.7	232.8
4. Transfer payments, net	-25.9	-25.2	-29.7	-29.1	-27.1	-29.1	-31.8	-33.8	-36.7	-59.2
of which:										
Remittances of foreign workers	-8.3	-8.3	-9.0	-8.0	-7.5	-7.4	-7.5	-7.6	-7.5	-7.0
Transfers to the European Community, net	-7.5	-6.0	-7.3	-8.3	-8.2	-10.4	-13.0	-13.4	-11.6	-19.1
Balance on current account	12.4	13.5	27.9	48.3	85.8	82.5	88.9	108.0	76.1	-32.9
B. Capital account										
1. Long-term capital transactions										
German investment abroad (increase:-)	-28.4	-36.5	-45.0	-61.7	-55.4	-62.2	-98.0	-95.0	-106.8	-92.9
Direct investment	-6.0	-8.1	-12.5	-14.1	-20.9	-16.4	-20.1	-27.3	-37.0	-35.7
Foreign securities	-11.4	-10.4	-15.7	-31.5	-21.3	-24.5	-72.6	-50.2	-23.5	-26.3
Advances and loans to non-residents	-8.7	-14.7	-14.2	-13.1	-10.3	-18.6	-2.5	-14.2	-43.0	-26.4
Other	-2.3	-3.3	-2.6	-3.0	-3.0	-2.7	-2.8	-3.3	-3.3	-4.4
Foreign investment in Germany (increase:+)	14.2	29.5	25.2	48.8	88.9	40.2	11.2	72.5	40.6	65.0
Direct investment	2.0	4.5	1.6	1.7	2.6	3.4	2.1	13.2	3.7	4.8
Domestic securities	12.2	13.6	17.4	38.3	74.1	33.9	7.6	45.2	17.1	64.0
Advances and loans to residents	0.1	11.6	6.2	8.9	12.3	2.9	1.7	14.3	20.1	-3.7
Other	-0.1	-0.2	-0.0	-0.1	-0.1	-0.1	-0.2	-0.1	-0.2	-0.1
Balance of long-term capital transactions	-14.2	-7.0	-19.8	-12.9	33.4	-22.0	-86.8	-22.5	-66.2	-27.9
2. Short-term capital transactions (net exports:-)										
Enterprises and individuals	3.2	-8.9	-16.1	-14.2	-56.7	-11.5	-21.4	-51.6	-19.—	7.1
Financial credits	5.1	-3.1	-7.4	-10.7	-51.5	-13.4	-13.0	-41.3	-17.—	12.0
Trade credits	-1.9	-5.9	-8.7	-3.5	-5.2	1.9	-8.4	-10.3	-1.1	-4.9

Official	-0.3	-4.3	-1.6	0.1	-0.3	1.0	0.8	-4.8	-5.2	-4.7
Banks	8.1	1.8	0.1	-27.7	-59.0	-6.6	-20.2	-56.7	0.6	39.8
Assets	4.3	5.3	-17.8	-33.4	-65.8	-15.4	-30.1	-81.0	-24.3	19.0
Liabilities	3.8	-3.6	17.8	5.7	6.8	8.9	9.9	24.3	24.9	20.8
Balance of short-term capital transactions	11.0	-11.5	-17.7	-41.7	-116.0	-17.0	-40.8	-113.0	-23.9	42.3
Balance on capital account	-3.2	-18.4	-37.5	-54.6	-82.6	-39.0	-127.5	-135.6	-90.1	14.4
C. Balancing item	-6.2	0.8	6.5	8.1	2.7	-2.2	3.9	8.6	25.0	18.8
D. Change in the net external assets of the Bundesbank (increase:+)	2.7	-1.6	-1.0	-1.3	2.8	31.9	-32.5	-21.6	5.9	0.8

Note: From July 1990 including the external transactions of the former German Democratic Republic.
Source: Deutsche Bundesbank, *Statistische Beihefte zu den Monatsberichten*, Reihe 3.

113

Table G. Imports and exports by regions - customs basis[1]

DM billion

	1981	1982	1983	1984	1985	1986	1987	1988	1989	1990	1991
Imports, cif											
OECD, total	271.853	279.983	297.968	330.157	357.009	331.199	331.932	355.215	408.607	446.031	515.456
EC	180.685	187.635	198.944	217.269	235.664	216.021	215.580	227.363	258.660	286.663	332.859
Belgium-Luxembourg	24.675	25.480	28.093	28.834	29.112	29.250	29.129	31.160	34.968	39.729	45.653
France	40.124	42.878	44.567	45.840	49.280	47.083	47.482	53.052	60.403	65.111	78.489
Italy	27.562	28.710	31.570	34.173	37.155	38.092	39.206	40.217	45.189	51.820	59.542
Netherlands	44.323	45.946	48.143	53.047	58.277	47.798	44.934	45.421	51.903	55.905	62.080
United Kingdom	27.502	27.002	27.138	33.286	37.164	29.758	29.364	30.443	34.687	37.042	42.394
Austria	10.279	11.115	12.604	13.727	15.350	16.383	17.293	18.917	20.995	23.941	26.486
Japan	12.910	12.647	14.819	18.306	20.720	24.030	25.245	28.366	32.143	32.841	39.564
Sweden	7.682	7.496	8.428	9.929	10.870	9.984	9.979	10.749	12.793	13.192	14.249
Switzerland	12.615	12.928	13.971	15.636	17.164	18.494	18.968	19.653	21.237	23.394	25.040
United States	28.388	28.213	27.712	31.097	32.341	26.864	25.613	29.095	38.265	36.924	42.903
Other OECD	19.294	19.949	21.490	24.193	24.900	19.423	19.254	21.072	24.514	29.124	34.355
Central and Eastern European countries[2]											26.443
Non-oil developing countries	40.590	42.298	42.784	50.378	53.392	48.159	47.138	53.107	60.354	60.887	64.387
OPEC	37.449	32.824	27.283	27.290	27.100	13.229	11.100	10.826	12.361	14.105	15.029
Centrally-planned economies[2]	19.287	21.359	22.157	26.432	26.310	21.157	19.471	20.461	25.143	7.714	11.739
Total imports	369.179	376.464	390.192	434.257	463.811	413.744	409.641	439.609	506.465	550.428	633.054
Exports, fob											
OECD, total	293.397	321.562	330.652	383.135	429.320	432.087	439.860	475.168	534.462	536.447	540.076
EC	194.911	216.020	217.677	243.638	267.264	267.455	277.916	308.195	352.668	350.442	357.002
Belgium-Luxembourg	28.907	31.082	31.849	34.018	39.967	37.712	38.846	42.040	45.979	47.755	48.161
France	51.910	60.129	55.564	61.336	64.001	62.331	63.609	71.272	84.314	83.835	86.827
Italy	31.306	32.376	32.088	37.663	41.795	42.879	46.056	51.652	59.807	59.998	60.872
Netherlands	33.884	36.144	37.857	42.125	46.254	45.458	46.088	49.189	54.395	54.315	55.357
United Kingdom	26.163	31.317	35.401	40.579	45.967	44.600	46.632	52.874	59.359	54.795	50.481
Austria	20.010	20.620	22.123	24.334	27.395	28.119	28.410	31.868	35.269	36.843	39.162
Japan	4.759	5.166	5.603	6.918	7.888	8.707	10.545	13.111	15.268	16.653	16.453
Sweden	10.427	11.350	11.271	12.796	14.734	14.747	15.842	16.650	18.353	17.453	14.674
Switzerland	20.728	21.968	22.376	25.872	28.856	31.033	32.126	34.442	38.147	37.443	37.448
United States	25.976	28.120	32.847	46.834	55.533	55.206	49.879	45.678	46.624	44.877	41.558
Other OECD	16.586	18.318	18.755	22.743	27.650	26.820	25.142	25.224	28.133	29.853	33.779

Central and Eastern European countries[2]	...	...	...	...	...	...	...	...	...	23.458	26.009
Non-oil developing countries	49.073	47.614	47.447	53.815	54.762	50.471	50.228	52.300	60.873	60.638	56.911
OPEC	34.883	38.043	31.577	27.948	25.199	17.913	14.295	15.463	16.400	18.200	21.272
Centrally-planned economies[2]	19.545	20.522	22.605	23.325	27.883	25.892	22.994	24.723	29.306	4.018	4.095
Total exports	396.898	427.741	432.281	488.223	537.164	526.363	527.377	567.654	641.041	642.785	648.363

1. From July 1990 including the external transactions of the former German Democratic Republic.
2. Until 1990 Central and Eastern European countries are included in centrally-planned economies.
Sources: Statistisches Bundesamt, *Wirtschaft und Statistik*; OECD, *Statistics of Foreign Trade, Series A*.

Table H. **Foreign trade by main commodity groups - customs basis**

DM billion

	1981	1982	1983	1984	1985	1986	1987	1988	1989	1990	1991
Imports, cif											
SITC classification											
0. Food and live animals	36.59	37.84	38.59	41.95	44.36	42.74	40.15	41.44	43.76	46.39	53.63
1. Beverages and tobacco	3.80	4.08	4.21	4.11	4.60	4.50	4.47	4.38	4.70	5.43	6.56
2. Crude materials, except fuels	26.33	26.06	27.12	31.0	31.88	26.50	25.11	28.51	33.54	29.55	28.64
3. Mineral fuels, lubricants and related materials	89.78	88.36	82.81	88.52	92.17	48.50	39.50	33.56	38.26	46.10	53.56
4. Animal and vegetable oils,etc...	1.73	1.74	1.86	2.95	2.75	1.52	1.17	1.45	1.73	1.52	1.61
5. Chemicals	27.47	29.16	31.89	37.02	41.27	38.35	38.51	42.62	47.69	49.71	54.16
6. Manufactured goods classified chiefly by material	59.20	59.29	63.45	71.28	74.93	73.40	71.64	80.47	94.63	98.37	106.69
7. Machinery and transport equipment	72.59	76.60	85.10	95.14	105.94	108.94	114.31	128.19	154.42	178.40	226.20
8. Miscellaneous manufactured articles	41.35	41.32	43.73	49.56	52.89	56.08	61.54	65.71	73.31	83.11	102.69
9. Other	10.35	9.02	9.17	9.84	10.38	10.81	10.96	13.38	14.56	13.10	11.70
0-9. Total imports	369.18	373.46	387.92	431.37	461.16	411.34	407.37	439.73	506.60	551.68	645.44
Exports, fob											
SITC classification											
0. Food and live animals	18.92	19.42	18.88	20.93	21.54	21.70	21.10	23.64	25.99	25.25	29.16
1. Beverages and tobacco	2.26	2.56	2.84	3.10	3.51	3.36	3.10	3.25	3.62	3.74	4.23
2. Crude materials, except fuels	7.98	7.59	8.10	9.81	10.72	9.23	9.24	10.64	12.37	11.75	12.48
3. Mineral fuels, lubricants and related materials	16.08	16.02	14.63	16.11	15.27	8.62	7.11	6.92	7.85	8.26	8.22
4. Animal and vegetable oils,etc...	1.76	1.71	1.73	2.57	2.80	1.69	1.32	1.60	1.82	1.55	1.52
5. Chemicals	49.45	51.37	56.76	66.27	71.16	67.69	68.56	76.93	83.08	81.97	84.71
6. Manufactured goods classified chiefly by material	76.93	80.21	80.16	91.18	100.34	95.13	93.38	102.54	117.16	113.82	113.25
7. Machinery and transport equipment	177.15	199.52	196.40	218.70	246.63	251.29	254.64	272.84	311.90	319.15	326.43
8. Miscellaneous manufactured articles	36.11	38.90	40.49	46.39	53.63	55.91	56.84	62.35	69.69	72.3	74.52
9. Other	9.90	8.09	10.69	11.10	9.72	9.94	10.68	6.96	7.78	8.43	11.64
0-9. Total exports	396.54	425.38	430.68	486.14	535.31	524.56	525.97	567.67	641.26	646.25	666.16

Note: Transactions with the former German Democratic Republic are not included. In 1991 western Germany only.
Source: OECD, *Statistics of Foreign Trade*, Series A.

Table I. Money and credit

End of period, DM billion

	1981	1982	1983	1984	1985	1986	1987	1988	1989	1990	1991
Consolidated balance sheet of the banking system:											
I. Bank lending to domestic non-banks	1 609.15	1 713.48	1 825.80	1 931.0	2 052.71	2 131.33	2 214.17	2 346.88	2 482.65	2 888.61	3 160.74
Bundesbank	17.11	15.43	17.33	15.39	12.93	16.77	13.91	14.52	13.87	13.53	13.67
Credit institutions	1 592.04	1 698.05	1 808.47	1 915.61	2 039.78	2 114.57	2 200.26	2 332.37	2 468.78	2 875.08	3 147.07
To public sector	368.80	408.70	427.94	446.84	467.07	471.62	500.49	541.43	547.23	604.11	629.31
To private sector	1 223.24	1 289.35	1 380.53	1 468.77	1 572.71	1 642.95	1 699.77	1 790.94	1 921.55	2 270.97	2 517.76
Short-term	291.27	303.65	317.99	340.19	350.14	342.06	325.81	341.47	374.07	520.76	575.87
Medium- and long-term	931.97	985.70	1 062.54	1 128.58	1 222.57	1 300.89	1 373.96	1 449.47	1 547.48	1 750.21	1 941.89
II. Net foreign assets	110.55	113.71	119.46	126.29	164.19	227.43	270.83	255.89	291.87	324.34	334.25
Bundesbank	65.78	68.45	66.52	65.28	64.49	67.70	99.77	67.11	45.79	51.81	52.55
Credit institutions	44.77	45.26	52.94	61.01	99.70	159.73	171.06	188.78	246.07	272.52	281.70
III. Domestic monetary capital holdings	897.27	945.49	1 015.86	1 093.01	1 184.15	1 265.97	1 339.49	1 369.57	1 482.80	1 671.34	1 852.91
Time deposits (more than 4-year notification)	230.94	238.37	265.60	291.87	327.37	362.39	406.25	452.62	491.31	524.87	560.10
Public sector	127.37	128.65	135.39	142.49	150.20	155.16	160.18	165.15	169.28	173.75	185.36
Private sector	103.57	109.72	130.21	149.38	177.17	207.23	246.07	287.47	322.03	351.12	374.74
Saving deposits and certificates	587.79	619.61	659.62	720.56	746.81	781.77	801.51	777.52	835.46	956.16	1 080.86
Share capital and reserves	78.54	87.51	90.63	98.58	109.97	121.81	131.73	139.43	156.03	190.34	211.95
IV. Public sector claims on the Bundesbank	0.77	1.26	2.16	0.98	2.25	1.14	4.66	3.54	6.88	19.15	12.72
V. Other items, net	-343.53	-378.24	-411.88	-420.98	-453.40	-480.72	-495.20	-533.58	-508.46	-535.13	-544.93
VI. Money and quasi-money (M2= I + II - III - IV + V)	478.13	502.20	515.36	542.32	577.10	610.93	645.65	696.08	776.38	987.30	1 084.43
VII. Time deposits (less than 4-year notification)	222.86	229.15	219.57	228.09	243.01	252.18	260.48	269.08	325.76	403.11	480.41
Money supply (M1 = VI - VII)	255.27	273.05	295.79	314.23	334.09	358.75	385.17	427.00	450.63	584.19	604.02
Sight deposits	171.08	184.41	199.37	214.43	230.23	246.59	261.08	284.40	303.71	425.62	432.25
Currency in circulation	84.19	88.64	96.43	99.80	103.87	112.15	124.09	142.60	146.92	158.57	171.77
Memorandum items:											
Central bank money[1]	164.70	174.60	186.30	195.0	203.80	220.70	238.80	259.0	271.70	...	339.10
M3	776.03	830.96	874.84	916.17	985.46	1 050.69	1 112.44	1 189.61	1 255.46	1 502.95	1 597.62

1. Defined as currency in circulation plus minimum reserves on domestic bank liabilities at current reserve ratios. Data reported here are averages of seasonally adjusted daily figures for December.

Source: Deutsche Bundesbank, *Monatsberichte*.

Table J. **Population and employment**

	1981	1982	1983	1984	1985	1986	1987	1988	1989	1990	1991[1]
	Thousands										
Population	61 682	61 638	61 423	61 175	61 024	61 066	61 077	61 449	62 063	63 253	..
Working-age population (15-64 years)	41 427	41 973	42 390	42 655	42 740	42 798	42 826	42 960	43 258	44 073	..
Labour force, total	28 305	28 558	28 605	28 659	28 897	29 188	29 386	29 608	29 771	30 327	30 575
Self-employed	3 126	3 086	3 054	3 042	3 034	3 050	3 016	3 001	2 980	2 963	2 978
Dependent employment, total	23 907	23 639	23 293	23 351	23 559	23 910	24 141	24 365	24 753	25 481	25 908
Nationals	21 995	21 852	21 599	21 742	21 991	22 340	22 564	22 755	23 075	23 706	..
Foreigners	1 912	1 787	1 694	1 609	1 568	1 570	1 577	1 610	1 678	1 775	..
Employment, total	27 033	26 725	26 347	26 393	26 593	26 960	27 157	27 366	27 733	28 444	28 886
	Per cent of civilian employment										
Agriculture, forestry, fishing	5.1	5.0	4.9	4.7	4.5	4.4	4.2	4.0	3.7	3.4	3.2
Industry	42.8	42.0	41.3	41.0	40.8	40.6	40.3	39.9	39.8	39.8	39.5
Commerce and communications	18.7	18.7	18.7	18.7	18.6	18.5	18.5	18.6	18.7	18.8	18.8
Other	33.4	34.3	35.1	35.6	36.1	36.5	37.0	37.5	37.8	38.0	38.5
	Thousands										
Unemployment	1 272	1 833	2 258	2 266	2 304	2 228	2 229	2 242	2 038	1 883	1 689
Short-time workers	347	606	675	384	235	197	278	208	108	56	145
Vacancies	208	105	76	88	110	154	171	189	251	314	331
	Per cent of dependent labour force										
Unemployment	5.5	7.5	9.1	9.1	9.3	9.0	8.9	8.7	7.9	7.5	6.3
Vacancies	1.0	0.5	0.3	0.4	0.4	0.6	0.7	0.7	1.0	1.5	1.1

1. Western Germany only.
Sources: Statistisches Bundesamt, *Wirtschaft und Statistik* and *Volkswirtschaftliche Gesamtrechnungen*, Reihe 1; Sachverständigenrat, *Jahresgutachten*; OECD *Labour Force Statistics*.

Table K. Wages and prices

Indices 1985=100

	1981	1982	1983	1984	1985	1986	1987	1988	1989	1990	1991
Wages and productivity, whole economy											
Monthly contractual pay rates	88.3	91.7	94.7	97.3	100.0	103.5	107.0	110.0	112.9	118.1	125.4
Monthly gross wages and salaries per employee	87.9	91.4	94.3	97.2	100.0	103.6	106.8	110.0	113.3	118.6	125.9
Output per employee	93.3	93.5	96.4	98.9	100.0	100.8	101.5	104.4	106.4	108.2	109.1
Unit labour costs[1]	93.2	97.0	97.5	98.3	100.0	102.8	105.3	105.4	106.4	109.2	114.6
Wages and productivity, manufacturing											
Hourly contractual pay rates, blue collar	85.7	89.6	92.6	95.2	100.0	103.7	108.2	112.4	116.6	121.5	129.5
Hourly gross earnings, blue collar	86.3	90.5	93.6	95.7	100.0	103.5	107.9	112.5	117.2	122.9	130.3
Hours worked, blue collar	108.2	103.5	99.9	99.2	100.0	100.9	99.4	99.5	101.3	103.0	103.1
Output per man-hour	88.0	88.7	92.3	95.9	100.0	101.5	103.6	108.0	112.0	116.1	119.9
Unit labour costs	96.5	100.2	99.2	99.0	100.0	103.6	106.7	106.3	107.5	110.4	114.9
Agricultural producer prices	103.3	107.0	105.4	104.1	100.0	94.3	91.7	91.8	99.8	94.7	94.0
Industrial producer prices	88.3	93.5	94.9	97.6	100.0	97.5	95.1	96.3	99.3	101.0	103.4
Costs of dwelling construction	92.5	95.1	97.1	99.6	100.0	101.4	103.3	105.5	109.4	116.4	124.3
GNP deflator	89.0	92.9	95.9	97.8	100.0	103.3	105.3	106.9	109.7	113.4	118.5
Private consumption deflator	88.3	92.6	95.6	98.0	100.0	99.5	100.1	101.5	104.6	107.3	111.1
Consumer prices											
Including food	88.0	92.6	95.7	98.0	100.0	99.9	100.1	101.4	104.2	107.0	110.7
Excluding food	87.4	91.8	95.0	97.6	100.0	99.7	100.1	101.7	104.7	107.4	111.3
Foreign trade prices											
Exports	88.7	92.5	94.1	97.4	100.0	98.2	97.3	99.3	102.1	102.2	103.5
Imports	91.3	93.4	93.1	98.6	100.0	84.3	79.8	80.8	84.4	82.5	82.8

1. Including mining and quarrying.
Source: Statistisches Bundesamt.

Table L. Structure of output and performance indicators

A. Structure of output (constant prices)

Share of GDP

	1986	1987	1988	1989	1990	1991
Agriculture, hunting, forestry and fishing	1.9	1.7	1.8	1.7	1.8	1.6
Energy, water supply, mining	3.5	3.6	3.5	3.5	3.4	3.3
Manufacturing	31.5	30.4	30.3	30.4	30.4	30.2
Construction	5.2	5.0	4.9	4.9	4.9	4.9
Traded services	27.2	27.7	27.9	28.1	28.1	28.5
Non-traded services	14.6	15.2	15.7	15.7	16.0	16.4
Total traded goods and services	83.9	83.7	84.1	84.4	84.5	84.9
General government non-traded sector	11.3	11.3	11.0	10.7	10.3	10.2

Share of total employment

	1986	1987	1988	1989	1990	1991
Agriculture, hunting, forestry and fishing	4.4	4.1	3.9	3.7	3.4	3.2
Energy, water supply, mining	1.8	1.8	1.8	1.7	1.6	1.6
Manufacturing	31.8	31.6	31.3	31.3	31.4	31.5
Construction	6.8	6.7	6.6	6.6	6.7	6.8
Traded services	21.4	21.5	21.6	21.7	21.8	19.2
Non-traded services	13.8	14.1	14.5	14.9	15.4	19.2
Total traded goods and services	80.0	79.8	79.8	79.9	80.4	81.5
General government non-traded sector	15.5	15.6	15.5	15.4	15.1	..

B. Economic performance (constant prices)

Productivity growth

	1986	1987	1988	1989	1990	1991
Agriculture, hunting, forestry and fishing	12.2	-4.7	12.2	8.6	12.4	-5.9
Energy, water supply, mining	-1.1	5.0	0.8	6.9	2.7	1.8
Manufacturing	-0.2	-2.0	3.3	2.3	1.7	0.9
Construction	2.8	-0.3	2.2	2.1	-0.0	-0.2
Traded services	2.0	1.8	3.2	2.3	1.3	..
Non-traded services	1.7	2.4	3.1	-0.4	0.4	..
Total traded goods and services	1.3	0.6	3.5	2.2	1.6	0.7
General government non-traded sector	-0.2	0.2	0.6	-0.4	0.9	..

Share of total investment

	1985	1986	1987	1988	1989	1990
Agriculture, hunting, forestry and fishing	2.6	2.5	2.5	2.5	2.4	..
Energy, water supply, mining	6.3	6.0	5.6	4.9	4.4	..
Manufacturing	19.5	20.0	19.5	19.8	20.0	..
Construction	1.2	1.2	1.2	1.4	1.5	..
Traded services	40.8	39.8	40.0	39.3	..	..
Non-traded services	16.2	17.3	18.5	19.7	.	..
Total traded goods and services	86.6	86.9	87.3	87.6	88.4	..
General government non-traded sector	11.9	11.6	11.3	11.0	10.3	..

C. Others indicators (current prices)

	1981	1982	1983	1984	1985	1986	1987	1988	1989	1990
Total R&D expenditure as % of total GDP	2.4	2.5	2.5	2.5	2.7	2.9	2.9	2.8	2.9	2.8
R&D as % of GDP in manufacturing sector	5.0	..	5.3	..	5.8	..	6.2	..	..	..
Government-funded R&D as % of total	40.7	40.8	38.8	37.9	36.7	35.3	34.7	34.2	34.1	34.1

Sources: Statistisches Bundesamt, *Volkswirtschaftliche Gesamtrechnungen*, Reihe 1; OECD, *Main Science and Technology Indicators.*

Table M. Labour market indicators

	A. TREND								
	Peak		Trough		1987	1988	1989	1990	1991
Standardised unemployment rate	1983:	8.0	1980:	3.0	6.2	6.2	5.6	7.9	4.3
Unemployment rate									
Total	1985:	9.3	1979:	3.8	8.9	8.7	7.9	7.2	6.3
Male	1985:	8.6	1979:	2.9	8.0	7.8	6.9	6.3	5.8
Female	1986:	10.6	1980:	5.2	10.2	10.0	9.4	8.4	7.0
Youth[1]	1983:	9.1	1980:	3.2	6.6	6.1	..	5.0	4.5
Share of long-term unemployment[2]	1980:	12.9	1988:	32.6	31.9	32.6	31.4	29.7	..
Registered vacancies (thousands)	1990:	314	1983:	76	171	189	251	314	331
Length of working week (1985=100)[3]	1985:	100.0	1989:	98.3	98.7	98.7	98.3	97.3	96.5

	B. STRUCTURAL AND INSTITUTIONAL FEATURES								
	1983	1984	1985	1986	1987	1988	1989	1990	1991
Labour force (% change)	0.2	0.2	0.8	1.0	0.7	0.8	0.6	1.8	1.9
Participation rate[4]									
Total	67.5	67.2	67.6	68.2	68.6	68.9	68.5	68.9	..
Males	83.5	82.8	83.0	83.0	82.7	82.8	82.2	..	..
Females	51.6	51.7	52.3	53.4	54.4	54.8	54.5	..	..
Employment/population from 15 to 64 years	60.9	60.6	61.0	61.8	62.2	62.5	..	..	..
Employers, self-employed and family workers (as % of total)	11.6	11.6	11.5	11.4	11.1	11.0	10.8	10.4	10.2
Wage-earners and salaried employees (as % of total)	88.4	88.4	88.5	88.6	88.9	89.0	89.2	89.6	89.8
Civilian employment by sector (% change)									
Agriculture	−3.3	−3.1	−3.5	−1.6	−4.4	−4.2	−6.0	−5.1	−3.2
Industry	−3.0	−0.5	0.2	0.8	−0.2	−0.2	1.2	3.0	1.8
Services	−0.1	1.2	1.6	2.1	1.9	2.0	2.0	3.4	3.5
of which: General government	0.7	0.3	1.3	1.6	1.1	0.5	0.6	0.7	..
Total	−1.5	0.2	0.7	1.4	0.7	0.8	1.4	2.9	2.6
Civilian employment by sector (as % of total)									
Agriculture	5.0	4.8	4.6	4.4	4.2	4.0	3.7	3.4	3.2
Industry	41.5	41.2	40.9	40.7	40.3	39.8	39.8	39.8	39.5
Services	53.5	54.0	54.5	54.9	55.5	56.2	56.5	56.8	57.3
of which: General government	15.4	15.5	15.5	15.6	15.6	15.6	15.5	15.1	15.1
Total	100.0	100.0	100.0	100.0	100.0	100.0	100.0	100.0	100.0
Short-time workers[5]	2.6	1.5	0.9	0.7	1.0	0.8	0.4	0.2	0.5
Non-wage labour costs[6]	18.5	18.8	18.8	18.8	18.8	18.9	18.8	18.6	18.6

1. 15-19 year old.
2. People looking for a job one year or more as a percentage of total unemployment.
3. Hours worked by wage-earners in manufacturing.
4. Labour force as a percentage of population from 15 to 64 years.
5. Short-time workers as percentage of total employment.
6. Employers' social security contributions as a percentage of total wage.
Sources: Statistisches Bundesamt; Bundesanstalt für Arbeit, *Amtliche Nachrichten,* Jahreszahlen; OECD, *National Accounts, Labour Force Statistics* and *Main Economic Indicators.*

	1985	1986	1987	1988	1989	1990
Budgetary indicators: general government accounts (% of GNP)						
Primary receipts (excluding interest)	44.8	44.2	44.0	43.4	44.0	42.6
Primary expenditure (excluding interest)	43.7	43.2	43.5	43.2	41.7	42.3
Primary budget balance	1.1	1.0	0.5	0.2	2.4	0.2
General government budget balance	–1.1	–1.3	–1.9	–2.1	0.2	–1.9
Structure of expenditure and taxes (% of GNP)						
General government expenditure	46.7	46.1	46.4	46.0	44.3	45.0
Consumption	19.9	19.8	19.8	19.6	18.7	18.3
Subsidies	2.1	2.1	2.2	2.3	2.1	2.0
Investment	2.3	2.4	2.4	2.3	2.3	2.3
General government receipts	45.5	44.8	44.5	43.9	44.5	43.1
Direct taxes	12.4	12.1	12.2	12.0	12.5	11.0
Indirect taxes	12.6	12.2	12.3	12.2	12.4	12.5
Social security contributions	17.4	17.4	17.5	17.4	17.0	16.9
Other indicators[1]						
Income tax as a per cent of total tax	41.3	41.6	42.8	42.1	42.4	40.1
Income tax elasticity	1.6	0.7	1.9	0.5	1.6	–0.4
Tax rates (%)						
Average effective personal income tax rate	19.2	18.8	19.3	19.1	20.1	..
Effective social security contribution rate	32.2	32.3	32.3	32.5	32.5	..
Standard VAT rate	14.0	14.0	14.0	14.0	14.0	14.0

1. Households.
Source: OECD, *National Accounts.*

Table O. **Financial markets**

	1970	1975	1980	1985	1987	1988	1989	1990	1991
Structure of financial flows[1]									
Share of intermediated financing in total financing	81.1	94.5	73.5	75.4	82.6	65.8	65.5	..	..
Financial institutions' share of financial assets	45.2	49.7	44.1	44.2	46.5	41.3	40.3	..	..
Structure of private non-financial sector's portfolio:									
Deposits[2]	73.3	74.7	57.9	60.9	61.8	50.9	44.7	..	..
Bonds and bills	12.0	7.9	14.3	15.0	14.2	20.6	23.3	..	..
Equities	4.8	3.8	4.1	2.8	3.7	4.4	-1.7	..	..
Non-financial corporate financial structure:	100.0	100.0	100.0	100.0	100.0	100.0	100.0	100.0	..
Own-financing	56.7	66.4	59.7	67.3	76.8	71.5	63.4	56.4	..
Debt and equity	37.0	22.5	32.9	26.8	15.3	22.5	31.2	32.1	..
Long-term debt	16.6	18.7	10.7	14.5	16.0	12.9	13.2	13.4	..
Equity	2.2	3.1	2.2	2.5	3.0	1.6	3.3	4.7	..
Short-term debt	18.2	0.7	20.0	9.8	-3.7	8.0	14.7	14.0	..
Other	6.3	11.1	7.4	5.9	8.0	6.1	5.4	4.2	..
Internationalisation of markets									
Foreign business of the banking sector[3]:									
Assets	6.5	7.1	7.4	8.8	10.3	10.8	12.3	11.8	11.5
Liabilities	4.1	4.0	6.1	5.7	5.6	5.9	6.4	6.5	6.4
International banking networks:									
Foreign banks in Germany[4]	..	44	88	118	122	160	164	177	175
German bank branches abroad	..	..	..	..	..	..	..	..	..
Share of long-term capital transactions:									
Net purchases of foreign securities by residents	..	..	0.6	30.4	31.0	2.2	19.1	8.3	26.0
Net purchases of domestic securities by non-residents	..	..	14.0	26.5	21.9	60.9	34.2	10.2	5.5
Efficiency of markets									
Divergence between Euro rates and domestic interest rates[5]	-1.0	-0.4	-0.4	-0.1	0.0	-0.1	-0.1	0.0	-0.1

1. Incomplete owing to lack of information on eastern Germany.
2. National and international means of payments plus other liquid assets.
3. As a percentage of deposit banks' balance sheets.
4. Number of branches and subsidaries.
5. Three-month Euro-DM interest rate minus three-month interbank rate.
Sources: Deutsche Bundesbank, *Monatsberichte* and *Statistische Beihefte*, Reihe 3 Zahlungsbilanzstatistik.

123

BASIC STATISTICS:

INTERNATIONAL COMPARISONS

	Units	Reference period[1]	Australia	Austria	Belgium
Population					
Total	Thousands	1989	16 833	7 624	9 938
Inhabitants per sq. km	Number	1989	2	91	326
Net average annual increase over previous 10 years	%	1989	1.5	0.1	0.1
Employment					
Total civilian employment (TCE)[2]	Thousands	1989	7 725	3 342	3 670
Of which: Agriculture	% of TCE		5.5	8.0	2.8
Industry	% of TCE		26.5	37.0	28.5
Services	% of TCE		68.0	55.1	68.7
Gross domestic product (GDP)					
At current prices and current exchange rates	Bill US $	1989	282.4	126.5	153.0
Per capita	US $		16 800	16 603	15 393
At current prices using current PPP's[3]	Bill US $	1989	240.4	102.1	135.0
Per capita	US $		14 304	13 407	13 587
Average annual volume growth over previous 5 years . . .	%	1989	3.9	2.7	2.6
Gross fixed capital formation (GFCF)	% of GDP	1989	25.5	24.0	19.1
Of which: Machinery and equipment	% of GDP		10.7	10.2	9.5
Residential construction	% of GDP		5.4	4.7	4.1
Average annual volume growth over previous 5 years . . .	%	1989	6.1	4.6	7.5
Gross saving ratio[4]	% of GDP	1989	22.5	26.0	20.9
General government					
Current expenditure on goods and services	% of GDP	1989	16.4	18.1	14.4
Current disbursements[5]	% of GDP	1989	32.1	44.9	53.3
Current receipts	% of GDP	1989	34.2	46.1	48.5
Net official development assistance	% of GNP	1989	0.38	0.23	0.43
Indicators of living standards					
Private consumption per capita using current PPP's[3] . . .	US $	1989	8 258	7 434	8 486
Passenger cars, per 1 000 inhabitants	Number	1988	435 (87)	370	349
Telephones, per 1 000 inhabitants	Number	1987	550 (85)	525	478
Television sets, per 1 000 inhabitants	Number	1986	472	323	301
Doctors, per 1 000 inhabitants	Number	1989	2.3 (86)	2.1	3.3 (88
Infant mortality per 1 000 live births	Number	1989	7.9	8.3	8.6
Wages and prices (average annual increase over previous 5 years)					
Wages (earnings or rates according to availability)	%	1989	5.3	4.7	2.9
Consumer prices	%	1989	7.8	2.2	2.4
Foreign trade					
Exports of goods, fob *	Mill US $	1989	37 191	32 448	100 081[7]
As % of GDP	%		13.2	25.7	65.4
Average annual increase over previous 5 years	%		10.0	15.6	14.0
Imports of goods, cif *	Mill US $	1989	40 981	38 902	98 586[7]
As % of GDP	%		14.5	30.8	64.4
Average annual increase over previous 5 years	%		12.7	14.7	12.2
Total official reserves[6]	Mill SDR's	1989	10 486	6 543	8 192[7]
As ratio of average monthly imports of goods	ratio		3.1	2.0	1.0

* At current prices and exchange rates.
1. Unless otherwise stated.
2. According to the definitions used in *OECD Labour Force Statistics*.
3. PPP's=Purchasing Power Parities.
4. Gross saving = Gross national disposable income minus Private and Government consumption.
5. Current disbursements = Current expenditure on goods and services plus current transfers and payments of property income.
6. Gold included in reserves is valued at 35 SDR's per ounce. End of year.
7. Including Luxembourg.

BASIC STATISTICS: INTERNATIONAL COMPARISONS

Canada	Denmark	Finland	France	Germany	Greece	Iceland	Ireland	Italy	Japan	Luxembourg	Netherlands	New Zealand	Norway	Portugal	Spain	Sweden	Switzerland	Turkey	United Kingdom	United States	Yugoslavia
248	5 132	4 964	56 160	61 990	10 033	253	3 515	57 525	123 120	378	14 849	3 343	4 227	10 337	38 888	8 493	6 723	55 255	57 236	248 762	23 690
3	119	15	102	249	76	2	50	191	326	145	364	12	13	112	77	19	163	71	234	27	93
1.0	0.0	0.4	0.5	0.1	0.5	1.1	0.4	0.2	0.6	0.4	0.6	0.6	0.4	0.5	0.5	0.2	0.6	2.4	0.2	1.0	0.8
486	2 610	2 460	21 484	27 208	3 671	140	1 077	20 833	61 280	181	6 065	1 461	2 014	4 377	12 260	4 466	3 518	16 771	26 457	117 342	..
4.3	5.7	8.9	6.4	3.7	25.3	10.0	15.1	9.3	7.6	3.3	4.7	10.3	6.6	19.0	13.0	3.6	5.6	50.1	2.1	2.9	..
25.7	27.4	30.9	30.1	39.8	27.5	30.7	28.4	32.4	34.3	31.5	26.5	25.4	25.3	35.3	32.9	29.4	35.1	20.5	29.4	26.7	..
70.1	66.9	60.2	63.5	56.5	47.1	59.3	56.5	58.2	58.2	65.2	68.8	64.3	68.1	45.7	54.0	67.0	59.3	29.5	68.4	70.5	..
645.5	106.2	115.5	958.2	1 189.1	54.2	5.2	33.9	865.8	2 869.3	7.0	223.7	41.7	90.2	45.3	380.3	189.9	177.2	79.1	837.5	5 132.0	81.8
783	20 685	23 270	17 061	19 182	5 399	20 516	9 644	15 051	23 305	18 613	15 063	12 503	21 341	4 623	9 711	22 360	26 350	1 432	14 642	20 629	3 454
506.7	74.9	74.6	818.0	929.0	72.8	4.0	31.6	799.7	1 934.4	6.5	203.6	38.2	69.4	72.1	401.2	131.7	119.0	247.4	820.6	5 132.0	..
305	14 594	15 030	14 565	14 985	7 253	15 870	8 984	13 902	15 712	17 192	13 709	11 446	16 422	7 360	10 244	15 511	17 699	4 481	14 345	20 629	..
3.9	2.0	4.0	2.7	2.6	2.2	3.1	3.2	3.1	4.5	4.4	2.4	0.8	2.2	4.3	4.2	2.3	3.0	5.1	3.8	3.6	..
22.2	18.2	27.6	20.8	20.5	18.5	18.7	18.4	20.2	31.0	24.1	21.8	21.0	27.5	26.2	24.0	21.2	27.6	22.8	19.6	16.6	14.5
7.5	8.0	10.9	9.3	9.3	8.0	5.1	9.9	10.6	13.0	10.9	10.6	10.5	9.4	9.8 (86)	8.5	9.6	9.5	11.7 (87)	9.4	7.8	..
7.4	4.2	7.7	5.1	5.3	4.6	4.3	3.6 (88)	4.8	6.1	4.3	5.5	4.9	4.1	4.8 (86)	4.9	5.2	18.1[9]	5.8 (87)	3.8	4.4	..
8.1	3.5	6.3	5.3	3.5	1.3	1.6	0.5	4.1	8.1	7.8	5.7	3.2	0.2	8.9	11.1	6.5	6.7	4.6	6.9	3.9	..
19.9	17.4	25.6	21.3	26.5	14.7	16.6	19.7	20.2	34.2	60.9	24.3	17.4	24.8	26.0	22.1	18.7	34.0	24.0	15.4	15.6	..
18.7	25.1	19.8	18.3	18.7	21.6	19.07	15.4	16.8	9.2	16.0	15.3	16.4	21.0	16.1	15.1	26.0	12.9	16.0	19.4	17.9	14.4
41.6	56.0	35.1	46.2	41.6	47.7	32.1	49.9 (87)	47.1	25.6	45.0 (86)	51.7	..	50.9	40.4 (86)	35.5 (88)	57.3	29.9	..	37.6	34.6	..
39.6	57.4	39.9	46.5	44.6	31.8	36.6	43.7 (87)	41.1	33.3	52.9 (86)	50.1	..	54.9	37.6 (86)	36.3 (88)	64.1	34.1	..	39.7	31.8	..
0.43	0.88	0.57	0.75	0.41	0.07	0.04	0.16	0.39	0.32	0.26	0.97	0.23	1.05	0.18	0.06	0.88	0.33	..	0.31	0.17	..
225	7 705	7 766	8 733	8 120	5 026	9 447	5 079	8 577	9 068	9 534	8 133	7 007	8 224	4 683	6 443	8 090	10 181	2 768	9 154	13 768	1 638*
454 (86)	321	344	394	457	130	488	210 (87)	408	241	443	348	490	388	190 (87)	263	400	419	20 (83)	318	559	129 (87)
780	864	617 (85)	608 (85)	650	413	525	265 (85)	488	555 (85)	425 (86)	639	697	622 (84)	202	396	890 (83)	856 (86)	91	524 (84)	650 (84)	154 (86)
546	386	372	332	379	174	306	216	255	585	253	327	358	348	157	322	393	411	165	534	813	176
2.2 (88)	2.7 (88)	2.0	2.6	3.0	3.2 (88)	2.7 (88)	1.5 (88)	1.3 (88)	1.6 (88)	1.9 (88)	2.4	1.9	2.5 (87)	2.8	3.7	3.1	2.9	0.8	1.4 (88)	2.3 (88)	1.8 (86)
7.2 (88)	7.5	6.1 (88)	7.5	7.5 (88)	9.9	5.3	7.6	8.9	4.6	9.9	6.8	10.8 (88)	8.3 (88)	12.2	7.8	5.8	7.3	6.5 (88)	8.4	9.7	24.8 (88)
3.9	6.0	7.6	3.9	4.1	16.1	..	6.1	6.9	3.3	..	2.1	9.2	9.0	15.6	8.8	7.9	..	..	8.4	2.7	220.8
4.3	4.3	4.9	3.6	1.3	17.1	23.7	3.7	6.2	1.1	1.8	0.7	11.2	6.6	12.6	6.9	5.6	2.1	50.6	5.3	3.6	210.2
7 154	28 113	23 279	179 192	340 987	7 595	1 429	20 782	140 596	274 266	..[8]	107 760	8 883	27 145	12 722	43 408	51 592	51 683	11 557	153 121	363 811	13 363
21.5	26.5	20.2	18.7	28.7	14.0	27.5	61.3	16.2	9.6	..	48.2	21.3	30.1	28.1	11.4	27.2	29.2	14.6	18.3	7.1	16.3
6.2	12.0	11.5	13.0	14.7	9.5	14.2	16.6	13.9	10.1	..	10.4	10.2	7.5	19.6	13.3	11.9	14.8	10.1	10.3	10.8	9.8
4 288	26 721	24 537	186 159	269 403	16 200	1 407	17 490	152 910	209 763	..	104 224	8 822	23 630	18 842	70 971	49 113	58 464	15 793	197 806	473 211	14 802
21	25.2	21.2	19.4	22.7	29.9	27.1	51.6	17.7	7.3	..	46.6	21.1	26.2	41.6	18.7	25.9	33.0	20.0	23.6	9.2	18.1
9.2	10.0	14.5	13.2	12.0	11.0	10.8	12.5	12.7	9.0	..	10.9	7.4	11.2	18.9	19.8	13.2	14.7	7.8	13.5	7.8	8.6
2 217	4 868	3 889	18 728	46 196	2 453	257	3 087	35 551	63 887	..	12 562	2 303	10 490	7 573	31 554	7 274	19 234	3 638	26 456	48 358	3 147
1.3	2.2	1.9	1.2	2.1	1.8	2.2	2.1	2.8	3.7	..	1.4	3.1	5.3	4.8	5.3	1.8	3.9	2.8	1.6	1.2	2.6

Included in Belgium.
Including non-residential construction.
Sources: Population and Employment: OECD Labour Force Statistics.
  GDP, GFCF, and General Government: OECD National Accounts, Vol. I and OECD Economic Outlook, Historical Statistics.
  Indicators of living standards: Miscellaneous national publications.
  Wages and Prices: OECD Main Economic Indicators.
  Foreign trade: OECD Monthly Foreign Trade Statistics, series A.
  Total official reserves: IMF International Financial Statistics.

August, 1991

EMPLOYMENT OPPORTUNITIES

Economics Department, OECD

The Economics Department of the OECD offers challenging and rewarding opportunities to economists interested in applied policy analysis in an international environment. The Department's concerns extend across the entire field of economic policy analysis, both macro-economic and micro-economic. Its main task is to provide, for discussion by committees of senior officials from Member countries, documents and papers dealing with current policy concerns. Within this programme of work, three major responsibilities are:

- to prepare regular surveys of the economies of individual Member countries;
- to issue full twice-yearly reviews of the economic situation and prospects of the OECD countries in the context of world economic trends;
- to analyse specific policy issues in a medium-term context for theOECD as a whole, and to a lesser extent for the non-OECD countries.

The documents prepared for these purposes, together with much of the Department's other economic work, appear in published form in the *OECD Economic Outlook, OECD Economic Surveys, OECD Economic Studies* and the Department's *Working Papers* series.

The Department maintains a world econometric model, INTERLINK, which plays an important role in the preparation of the policy analyses and twice-yearly projections. The availability of extensive cross-country data bases and good computer resources facilitates comparative empirical analysis, much of which is incorporated into the model.

The Department is made up of about 75 professional economists from a variety of backgrounds and Member countries. Most projects are carried out by small teams and last from four to eighteen months. Within the Department, ideas and points of view are widely discussed; there is a lively professional interchange, and all professional staff have the opportunity to contribute actively to the programme of work.

Skills the Economics Department is looking for:

a) Solid competence in using the tools of both micro-economic and macro-economic theory to answer policy questions. Experience indicates that this normally requires the equivalent of a PH.D. in economics or substantial relevant professional experience to compensate for a lower degree.

b) Solid knowledge of economic statistics and quantitative methods; this includes how to identify data, estimate structural relationships, apply basic techniques of time series analysis, and test hypotheses. It is essential to be able to interpret results sensibly in an economic policy context.

c) A keen interest in and knowledge of policy issues, economic developments and their political/social contexts.

d) Interest and experience in analysing questions posed by policy-makers and presenting the results to them effectively and judiciously. Thus, work experience in government agencies or policy research institutions is an advantage.

e) The ability to write clearly, effectively, and to the point. The OECD is a bilingual organisation with French and English as the official languages. Candidates must have excellent knowledge of one of those languages, and some knowledge of the other. Knowledge of other languages might also be an advantage for certain posts.

f) For some posts, expertise in a particular area may be important, but a successful candidate is expected to be able to work on a broader range of topics relevant to the work of the Department. Thus, except in rare cases, the Department does not recruit narrow specialists.

g) The Department works on a tight time schedule and strict deadlines. Moreover, much of the work in the Department is carried out in small groups of economists. Thus, the ability to work with other economists from a variety of cultural and professional backgrounds, to supervise junior staff, and to produce work on time is important.

General Information

The salary for recruits depends on educational and professional background. Positions carry a basic salary from FF 262 512 or FF 323 916 for Administrators (economists) and from FF 375 708 for Principal Administrators (senior economists). This may be supplemented by expatriation and/or family allowances, depending on nationality, residence and family situation. Initial appointments are for a fixed term of two to three years.

Vacancies are open to candidates from OECD Member countries. The Organisation seeks to maintain an appropriate balance between female and male staff and among nationals from Member countries.

For further information on employment opportunities in the Economics Department, contact:

Administrative Unit
Economics Department
OECD
2, rue André-Pascal
75775 PARIS CEDEX 16
FRANCE

Applications citing "ECSUR", together with a detailed *curriculum vitae* in English or French, should be sent to the Head of Personnel at the above address.

MAIN SALES OUTLETS OF OECD PUBLICATIONS
PRINCIPAUX POINTS DE VENTE DES PUBLICATIONS DE L'OCDE

ARGENTINA – ARGENTINE
Carlos Hirsch S.R.L.
Galería Güemes, Florida 165, 4° Piso
1333 Buenos Aires   Tel. (1) 331.1787 y 331.2391
                        Telefax: (1) 331.1787

AUSTRALIA – AUSTRALIE
D.A. Book (Aust.) Pty. Ltd.
648 Whitehorse Road, P.O.B 163
Mitcham, Victoria 3132   Tel. (03) 873.4411
                        Telefax: (03) 873.5679

AUSTRIA – AUTRICHE
Gerold & Co.
Graben 31
Wien I   Tel. (0222) 533.50.14

BELGIUM – BELGIQUE
Jean De Lannoy
Avenue du Roi 202
B-1060 Bruxelles   Tel. (02) 538.51.69/538.08.41
                        Telefax: (02) 538.08.41

CANADA
Renouf Publishing Company Ltd.
1294 Algoma Road
Ottawa, ON K1B 3W8   Tel. (613) 741.4333
                        Telefax: (613) 741.5439
Stores:
61 Sparks Street
Ottawa, ON K1P 5R1   Tel. (613) 238.8985
211 Yonge Street
Toronto, ON M5B 1M4   Tel. (416) 363.3171
Les Éditions La Liberté Inc.
3020 Chemin Sainte-Foy
Sainte-Foy, PQ G1X 3V6   Tel. (418) 658.3763
                        Telefax: (418) 658.3763

Federal Publications
165 University Avenue
Toronto, ON M5H 3B8   Tel. (416) 581.1552
                        Telefax: (416) 581.1743

CHINA – CHINE
China National Publications Import
Export Corporation (CNPIEC)
P.O. Box 88
Beijing   Tel. 403.5533
                        Telefax: 401.5664

DENMARK – DANEMARK
Munksgaard Export and Subscription Service
35, Nørre Søgade, P.O. Box 2148
DK-1016 København K   Tel. (33) 12.85.70
                        Telefax: (33) 12.93.87

FINLAND – FINLANDE
Akateeminen Kirjakauppa
Keskuskatu 1, P.O. Box 128
00100 Helsinki   Tel. (358 0) 12141
                        Telefax: (358 0) 121.4441

FRANCE
OECD/OCDE
Mail Orders/Commandes par correspondance:
2, rue André-Pascal
75775 Paris Cedex 16   Tel. (33-1) 45.24.82.00
Telefax: (33-1) 45.24.85.00 or (33-1) 45.24.81.76
                        Telex: 620 160 OCDE

OECD Bookshop/Librairie de l'OCDE :
33, rue Octave-Feuillet
75016 Paris   Tel. (33-1) 45.24.81.67
                        (33-1) 45.24.81.81

Documentation Française
29, quai Voltaire
75007 Paris   Tel. 40.15.70.00

Gibert Jeune (Droit-Économie)
6, place Saint-Michel
75006 Paris   Tel. 43.25.91.19

Librairie du Commerce International
10, avenue d'Iéna
75016 Paris   Tel. 40.73.34.60
Librairie Dunod
Université Paris-Dauphine
Place du Maréchal de Lattre de Tassigny
75016 Paris   Tel. 47.27.18.56
Librairie Lavoisier
11, rue Lavoisier
75008 Paris   Tel. 42.65.39.95
Librairie L.G.D.J. - Montchrestien
20, rue Soufflot
75005 Paris   Tel. 46.33.89.85
Librairie des Sciences Politiques
30, rue Saint-Guillaume
75007 Paris   Tel. 45.48.36.02
P.U.F.
49, boulevard Saint-Michel
75005 Paris   Tel. 43.25.83.40
Librairie de l'Université
12a, rue Nazareth
13100 Aix-en-Provence   Tel. (16) 42.26.18.08
Documentation Française
165, rue Garibaldi
69003 Lyon   Tel. (16) 78.63.32.23

GERMANY – ALLEMAGNE
OECD Publications and Information Centre
Schedestrasse 7
D-W 5300 Bonn 1   Tel. (0228) 21.60.45
                        Telefax: (0228) 26.11.04

GREECE – GRÈCE
Librairie Kauffmann
Mavrokordatou 9
106 78 Athens   Tel. 322.21.60
                        Telefax: 363.39.67

HONG-KONG
Swindon Book Co. Ltd.
13–15 Lock Road
Kowloon, Hong Kong   Tel. 366.80.31
                        Telefax: 739.49.75

ICELAND – ISLANDE
Mál Mog Menning
Laugavegi 18, Pósthólf 392
121 Reykjavik   Tel. 162.35.23

INDIA – INDE
Oxford Book and Stationery Co.
Scindia House
New Delhi 110001   Tel.(11) 331.5896/5308
                        Telefax: (11) 332.5993
17 Park Street
Calcutta 700016   Tel. 240832

INDONESIA – INDONÉSIE
Pdii-Lipi
P.O. Box 4298
Jakarta 12042   Tel. 583467
                        Telex: 62 875

IRELAND – IRLANDE
TDC Publishers – Library Suppliers
12 North Frederick Street
Dublin 1   Tel. 74.48.35/74.96.77
                        Telefax: 74.84.16

ISRAEL
Electronic Publications only
Publications électroniques seulement
Sophist Systems Ltd.
71 Allenby Street
Tel-Aviv 65134   Tel. 3-29.00.21
                        Telefax: 3-29.92.39

ITALY – ITALIE
Libreria Commissionaria Sansoni
Via Duca di Calabria 1/1
50125 Firenze   Tel. (055) 64.54.15
                        Telefax: (055) 64.12.57
Via Bartolini 29
20155 Milano   Tel. (02) 36.50.83
Editrice e Libreria Herder
Piazza Montecitorio 120
00186 Roma   Tel. 679.46.28
                        Telefax: 678.47.51
Libreria Hoepli
Via Hoepli 5
20121 Milano   Tel. (02) 86.54.46
                        Telefax: (02) 805.28.86
Libreria Scientifica
Dott. Lucio de Biasio 'Aeiou'
Via Coronelli, 6
20146 Milano   Tel. (02) 48.95.45.52
                        Telefax: (02) 48.95.45.48

JAPAN – JAPON
OECD Publications and Information Centre
Landic Akasaka Building
2-3-4 Akasaka, Minato-ku
Tokyo 107   Tel. (81.3) 3586.2016
                        Telefax: (81.3) 3584.7929

KOREA – CORÉE
Kyobo Book Centre Co. Ltd.
P.O. Box 1658, Kwang Hwa Moon
Seoul   Tel. 730.78.91
                        Telefax: 735.00.30

MALAYSIA – MALAISIE
Co-operative Bookshop Ltd.
University of Malaya
P.O. Box 1127, Jalan Pantai Baru
59700 Kuala Lumpur
Malaysia   Tel. 756.5000/756.5425
                        Telefax: 755.4424

NETHERLANDS – PAYS-BAS
SDU Uitgeverij
Christoffel Plantijnstraat 2
Postbus 20014
2500 EA's-Gravenhage   Tel. (070 3) 78.99.11
Voor bestellingen: Tel. (070 3) 78.98.80
                        Telefax: (070 3) 47.63.51

NEW ZEALAND
NOUVELLE-ZÉLANDE
Legislation Services
P.O. Box 12418
Thorndon, Wellington   Tel. (04) 496.5652
                        Telefax: (04) 496.5698

NORWAY – NORVÈGE
Narvesen Info Center – NIC
Bertrand Narvesens vei 2
P.O. Box 6125 Etterstad
0602 Oslo 6   Tel. (02) 57.33.00
                        Telefax: (02) 68.19.01

PAKISTAN
Mirza Book Agency
65 Shahrah Quaid-E-Azam
Lahore 3   Tel. 66.839
                        Telex: 44886 UBL PK. Attn: MIRZA BK

PORTUGAL
Livraria Portugal
Rua do Carmo 70-74
Apart. 2681
1117 Lisboa Codex   Tel.: (01) 347.49.82/3/4/5
                        Telefax: (01) 347.02.64

SINGAPORE – SINGAPOUR
Information Publications Pte
Golden Wheel Bldg.
41, Kallang Pudding, #04-03
Singapore 1334   Tel. 741 5166
                                           Telefax: 742.9356

SPAIN – ESPAGNE
Mundi-Prensa Libros S.A.
Castelló 37, Apartado 1223
Madrid 28001   Tel. (91) 431.33.99
                             Telefax: (91) 575.39.98

Libreria Internacional AEDOS
Consejo de Ciento 391
08009 – Barcelona   Tel. (93) 488.34.92
                             Telefax: (93) 487.76.59
Llibreria de la Generalitat
Palau Moja
Rambla dels Estudis, 118
08002 – Barcelona
                (Subscripcions) Tel. (93) 318.80.12
                (Publicacions) Tel. (93) 302.67.23
                             Telefax: (93) 412.18.54

SRI LANKA
Centre for Policy Research
c/o Colombo Agencies Ltd.
No. 300-304, Galle Road
Colombo 3   Tel. (1) 574240, 573551-2
                     Telefax: (1) 575394, 510711

SWEDEN – SUÈDE
Fritzes Fackboksföretaget
Box 16356
Regeringsgatan 12
103 27 Stockholm   Tel. (08) 23.89.00
                             Telefax: (08) 20.50.21

Subscription Agency-Agence d'abonnements
Wennergren-Williams AB
Nordenflychtsvägen 74
Box 30004
104 25 Stockholm   Tel. (08) 13.67.00
                             Telefax: (08) 618.62.32

SWITZERLAND – SUISSE
Maditec S.A. (Books and Periodicals - Livres
et périodiques)
Chemin des Palettes 4
1020 Renens/Lausanne   Tel. (021) 635.08.65
                             Telefax: (021) 635.07.80

Mail orders only - Commandes
par correspondance seulement
Librairie Payot
C.P. 3212
1002 Lausanne   Telefax: (021) 311.13.92

Librairie Unilivres
6, rue de Candolle
1205 Genève   Tel. (022) 320.26.23
                             Telefax: (022) 329.73.18

Subscription Agency – Agence d'abonnement
Naville S.A.
38 avenue Vibert
1227 Carouge   Tél.: (022) 308.05.56/57
                             Telefax: (022) 308.05.88

See also – Voir aussi :
OECD Publications and Information Centre
Schedestrasse 7
D-W 5300 Bonn 1 (Germany)
                             Tel. (49.228) 21.60.45
                             Telefax: (49.228) 26.11.04

TAIWAN – FORMOSE
Good Faith Worldwide Int'l. Co. Ltd.
9th Floor, No. 118, Sec. 2
Chung Hsiao E. Road
Taipei   Tel. (02) 391.7396/391.7397
                             Telefax: (02) 394.9176

THAILAND – THAÏLANDE
Suksit Siam Co. Ltd.
113, 115 Fuang Nakhon Rd.
Opp. Wat Rajbopith
Bangkok 10200   Tel. (662) 251.1630
                             Telefax: (662) 236.7783

TURKEY – TURQUIE
Kültur Yayinlari Is-Türk Ltd. Sti.
Atatürk Bulvari No. 191/Kat. 13
Kavaklidere/Ankara   Tel. 428.11.40 Ext. 2458
Dolmabahce Cad. No. 29
Besiktas/Istanbul   Tel. 160.71.88
                             Telex: 43482B

UNITED KINGDOM – ROYAUME-UNI
HMSO
Gen. enquiries   Tel. (071) 873 0011
Postal orders only:
P.O. Box 276, London SW8 5DT
Personal Callers HMSO Bookshop
49 High Holborn, London WC1V 6HB
                             Telefax: (071) 873 8200
Branches at: Belfast, Birmingham, Bristol, Edin-
burgh, Manchester

UNITED STATES – ÉTATS-UNIS
OECD Publications and Information Centre
2001 L Street N.W., Suite 700
Washington, D.C. 20036-4910 Tel. (202) 785.6323
                             Telefax: (202) 785.0350

VENEZUELA
Libreria del Este
Avda F. Miranda 52, Aptdo. 60337
Edificio Galipán
Caracas 106   Tel. 951.1705/951.2307/951.1297
                       Telegram: Libreste Caracas

YUGOSLAVIA – YOUGOSLAVIE
Jugoslovenska Knjiga
Knez Mihajlova 2, P.O. Box 36
Beograd   Tel. (011) 621.992
                             Telefax: (011) 625.970

Orders and inquiries from countries where Distribu-
tors have not yet been appointed should be sent to:
OECD Publications Service, 2 rue André-Pascal,
75775 Paris Cedex 16, France.

Les commandes provenant de pays où l'OCDE n'a
pas encore désigné de distributeur devraient être
adressées à : OCDE, Service des Publications,
2, rue André-Pascal, 75775 Paris Cedex 16, France.

Subscription to OECD periodicals may also be
placed through main subscription agencies.

Les abonnements aux publications périodiques de
l'OCDE peuvent être souscrits auprès des
principales agences d'abonnement.

PRINTED IN FRANCE

•

OECD PUBLICATIONS
2 rue André Pascal
75775 PARIS CEDEX 16
No. 46203
(10 92 15 1) ISBN 92-64-13744-0
ISSN 0376-6438

•